In order to write this exclusive story

LESTER DAVID and JHAN ROBBINS

talked with more than two hundred relatives, friends, and enemies of Jackie and Ari. They pored through many dozens of personal documents and papers. They visited the lush island of Skorpios—Onassis' fortress-playground, vacation spot for Beautiful People, and forbidden territory for almost everyone else.

They take you aboard the floating palace *Christina*, with its gold-fitted bathrooms and mosaic swimming pool. They describe fabulous parties with such celebrated guests as Winston Churchill and Liz Taylor. They tell how famous people reacted to the surprise marriage. And they fill in the backgrounds of this sensational couple to explain the attraction between two such complex and dissimilar people.

JACKIE AND ARI
is an original POCKET BOOK edition.

LESTER DAVID AND JHAN ROBBINS

JACKIE
AND ARI

PUBLISHED BY POCKET BOOKS NEW YORK

JACKIE AND ARI

POCKET BOOK edition published February, 1976

*Photos courtesy of Nicholas Tsikourias Greek Photo Agency,
Athens, and Keystone Press Agency, Inc., New York*

L

This original POCKET BOOK edition is printed from brand-new plates made from newly set, clear, easy-to-read type.
POCKET BOOK editions are published by POCKET BOOKS,
a division of Simon & Schuster, Inc., 630 Fifth Avenue,
New York, N.Y. 10020. Trademarks registered
in the United States and other countries.

Printed in the U.S.A.

Contents

Contents

Photo insert appears between pages 96 and 97.

JACKIE
AND ARI

Prologue

Nikos Kominates is a short, heavily muscled young Greek with a round handsome face that creases easily into a broad smile. He is sitting at one of the seven wooden tables in his waterfront taverna in Nidri on the Ionian Sea, remembering his friends, Jacqueline and Aristotle Onassis.

Skorpios, the late multimillionaire's island estate, lies less than two miles to the east. Shade your eyes against the glare of the sun on the blue-green water and you can see, dimly in the distance, the profile of the white *Christina,* Onassis' superbly appointed yacht, and on either side of her the outlines of the island itself. Onassis made the crossing frequently in a launch, his seamen drawing up close to Nikos' twenty-five-foot fishing boat, which lapped at anchor a dozen feet from the entrance to his taverna.

Onassis would leap nimbly to shore and greet his friend, and the two would sit at one of the tables facing the sea. Nikos would pour the ouzo, the clear ninety-proof national Greek drink that turns cloudy when mixed with water, and they would look out at passing boats and talk. It was simple talk—of the fishing, the weather, children, some old person's sickness, not of great tankers sailing to the ports of the world or of million-dollar deals.

We visited Nikos not long after his friend died and was buried on Skorpios, and sat at the same table where he had spent so many hours with Onassis.

It was early afternoon of a June day; the sky was a perfect blue, a soft breeze was coming in from the sea. Nikos remarked upon the beauty of the day as he poured us a drink. It was a "Jackie and Ari,"* a strange-tasting cocktail still enjoying considerable popularity in Greek restaurants and nightclubs. It combined ouzo, for the powerful Onassis, and a light, white French wine, representing the cultured Jackie. (In some clubs, the ouzo and wine were served in separate glasses; one quaffed the more potent brew and followed it with a wine chaser.)

Hardly anyone stirred in Nidri, which, although it's only a sleepy fishing village, is the chief port of the island of Lefkas off the western coast of Greece. Several children—sturdy, brown-legged, barefoot—played at the dockside. From down the street came the faint aroma of baking bread. Nikos' sister owns a shop where she makes the large, oblong rolls, golden in color and incredibly light in texture, that Jackie adored. Batches would be delivered to Skorpios regularly.

As we sipped our drinks, Nikos (who speaks English reasonably well but slips in Greek words when he cannot find their equivalent) asked, "He still be alive today if he not marry with her? *Ti nomízis?*—what

---

* His relatives and friends also called him "Aristo" or "Telis," diminutives for Aristotelis, his full name in Greek. To the French, he was "Daddy-O," but for most Americans, he was Ari, and we will call him that in this book. Onassis once remarked that Americans must have thought he was Irish—"'Arry O'Nassis."

you think? He try too hard to keep up with much younger woman? I hear some people talk that.

"But I no think so. Because I see with my own two eyes she give him happy times. Maybe not so many, but more than few. You understand?

"At funeral, I see how sad she be because he live no more. I can tell, she no acting. Sometimes I also see them argue. But I don't know. Nobody know. Jackie and Ari—*pánta ítan éna polí megálo mistírio*—always were big mystery."

Nikos remembered something else.

Affixed to the stern of his fishing boat was a wooden plaque bearing the likeness of a happy face. He had liked this face because it smiled upon the world, so he had attached it to his boat for all to see. It bobbed gently up and down at the dock, its smile constant.

Not once but several times, Nikos recalled, Onassis had pointed to the plaque and said, "Ah, Nikos. There are two happy people, you and that face."

The cryptic remark raises many questions.

Was Onassis seeing the happy faces of his friend, and the happy wooden one, as apart from himself? Was he thinking that those faces did not have his burdens, responsibilities, and anxieties? Was the contrast between the shining openness of the faces and his own life so sharp? Could it be that Aristotle Onassis, the man who possessed, or could possess, every kind of material thing, who was married to a woman many considered to be the uncrowned queen of the world, was confessing his essential unhappiness to a simple Greek tavern keeper whose life he may have envied?

After interviewing more than two hundred of the Onassises' friends, and enemies, and poring through many dozens of personal documents, we have discovered some answers that shed light upon what must be considered the most intriguing marriage/merger of the century. The romance between Wallis Warfield Simpson and Edward VIII of England was surely more significant historically—a throne was vacated for love of a woman—but the world was not perplexed by the "why" of the young monarch's action as it was—and still is—by the marriage between the world's most fascinating woman* and the world's richest man.**

Our investigation took us aboard the superyacht *Christina,* to the island kingdom of Skorpios, and to Athens, London, Paris, and Monaco. In the United States, we talked to many friends of the couple in New York, Washington, Boston, Chicago, and Los Angeles. Many were willing to be quoted by name.

Many persons, especially those in Nidri who had worked for Jackie and Ari or had served them in some capacity and thus had an exceptional opportunity to observe the couple closely, talked willing and extensively. In fact, it was often hard to stop them! Some, understandably enough, asked that their names be omitted.

Others who talked to us are members of Jackie's circle and, aware of her passion for privacy, do not wish to jeopardize their friendship with her, but at the same time want the truth to be known. Still others are doing business with the Onassis empire and fear the consequences of telling what they feel he might not have wanted told. These people prefer to be anonymous, and we have respected their wishes.

---

* Six consecutive Gallup polls listed Jackie as number one of the ten most admired women in the world.

** Some financial experts didn't list Onassis in first place, but all agreed that he certainly belonged well up there. He owned tankers, banks, real estate, an airline, and numerous other worldwide projects.

We sought answers to the questions asked repeatedly: Did Jackie marry Ari because of his wealth? Did he marry Jackie because she was the glamorous widow of the thirty-fifth president of the United States? How could such diametric opposites possibly stay married? What was this strange union like? How did the parties regard their marriage? What was the true relationship of Onassis' children, Christina and Alexander, to their stepmother? Could Onassis possibly be a substitute father to Caroline and John? How did the Kennedy clan regard the marriage? And, now that Jackie has been widowed twice, what about the future?

Here is what we uncovered as we closely examined this modern Greek tragedy. Many of these revealing facts and the stories of many of these incidents have never appeared in print before.

CHAPTER I

"Cards Don't Lie"

As 1962 drew to a close, Madame Ella, a Washington card-reading psychic, took a long look into the future. Madame Ella had acquired a degree of local fame as a seeress; a sign in her window bore the legend: "Near 100-percent accuracy in forecasting the future."

This time she made a prediction more startling than any she'd ever made before. "Jackie Kennedy," she announced, "will very soon meet a tall, dark, handsome, charming stranger with lots and lots of money." Nor did she stop there. "My cards tell me," she continued, "that she will marry this man."

Madame Ella's forecast was broadcast on New Year's Day by several radio stations, but they hardly took it seriously. Madame Ella had failed to mention death or divorce in her prediction, and many sarcastic letters were received by the radio stations. Most listeners wondered: "Won't President Kennedy mind?"

Evidently John Kennedy did indeed mind when his wife met someone who wasn't tall, dark and handsome, but otherwise answered Madame Ella's description. His wrath surfaced in a number of caustic phone and cable messages that he sent to Jackie during her much-publicized cruise on the *Christina* in the company of Onassis in the summer of 1963. (One of the milder admonitions the president cabled to Jackie was: "What I'd like to see in the headlines is a little more about Caroline and a little less about Onassis."

When the Golden Greek, as he was often called, was told about Madame Ella's prediction—made years before the Jackie-Ari marriage—he said matter-of-factly, "Do you think the fortune-teller really had me in mind? After all, she did say a stranger, and I was introduced to Mrs. Kennedy several years ago." Then he laughed as he added, "But I suppose that Tarot cards don't lie."

Shortly after Jackie's cruise on the *Christina,* President Kennedy was assassinated in Dallas, and a grieving world watched his heroic widow throughout the long and moving funeral ceremony. Nearly everyone's heart went out to the bereaved First Lady.* And "everyone" included Aristotle Onassis, who, upon hearing the sad news, immediately flew to Washington to offer his personal condolences. He was promptly invited to the White House—he was the first "outsider" to receive such an invitation—and grateful Jackie thanked him for his concern. She knew that the concern was shared by millions and remarked to a close friend, "I suppose that now I can get away with anything—that is, anything but marrying Eddie Fisher." **

For the next five years, Jackie played cat-and-mouse on the subject of marriage. She'd tell intimates in her little-girl voice, "The only way to live a full, natural life is with a husband." But a day later, she'd say,

---

* Said General Charles de Gaulle, "She gave an example to the whole world of how to behave." Even hardbitten newsmen called her "sublime."
** Poor Eddie Fisher was singled out twice. Jackie uttered nearly the same sentiments when she tried to censor William Manchester's book, *Death of a President.* At the time, Jackie said, "Anyone who gets in a fight with me will look like a rat unless I run off with Eddie Fisher."

"I've been married once—why chance it again?"

She dated men who were supposedly "safe" and who didn't present any marriage problems, men like the married composer Leonard Bernstein. She told the press her escorts were "just good friends." They included Onassis, historian Arthur Schlesinger, Jr., director Mike Nichols, writers Truman Capote and Philip Roth, and U.N. Ambassador Adlai Stevenson.

Jackie refused to make a fuss over any of her escorts. A friend in Washington said, "None of the men Jackie went out with were her special cup of tea. Her blend is exotic, rich, and different."

The only semiserious candidate seemed to be Lord Harlech, formerly David Ormsby-Gore, British ambassador to the United States. He accompanied Jackie on a trip to Cambodia, and there was a great deal of speculation that the two would eventually marry. But evidently he was not her "cup of tea" either.

Early in 1968, Jackie had several dates with "good friend" Aristotle Onassis. They were seen having an animated conversation in New York at the Colony and laughing at "21." On Easter Sunday, Ari and Jackie dined at Mykonos, a Greek restaurant in Manhattan. The guests included dancers Margot Fonteyn, Rudolf Nureyev, and Onassis' daughter, Christina.

A few months later, Jackie, chaperoned by brother-in-law Ted Kennedy, went off to Skorpios and then took a Caribbean cruise aboard the *Christina*. The Onassis charm took hold, and Jackie told another brother-in-law, Robert Kennedy, that she was very smitten with the Greek shipping magnate. Bobby, who exercised strong influence on her, didn't like the news and advised her to "cool it."

The romance, however, had reached a simmering point. Onassis had previously decided that Jackie

17

should be his new wife, and the Golden Greek usually had his way. When they were apart, he phoned daily and sent dozens of roses and small diamond trinkets. Occasionally he enclosed a note that said, "Giving is a king's pleasure." Jackie was an excellent receiver and thanked him profusely.

Ari spent several weekends at Hyannisport to become better acquainted with Caroline and John. He also met Jackie's mother and stepfather, Janet and Hugh D. Auchincloss, in Newport, and was introduced to various members of the Kennedy family. After meeting them, he confided to friends, "They're so talkative, they could almost be Greeks."

One of Ari's prime concerns was to establish good relationships with Jackie's children. It had been a long time since Onassis had been close to youngsters that age. One afternoon, he asked an aide in his New York office, "What do you do with an eleven-year-old girl and an eight-year-old boy?" The aide was silent. Ari thought a moment, and then said to the aide: "Go down to Scribner's and get all the books they got on bringing up growing children. And make sure you find one on stepfathers."

Soon the aide returned with a dozen volumes. One was *The Child from Ten to Sixteen,* by doctors Arnold Gesell and Frances L. Ilg of the famous Gesell Institute of Child Development. Another contained a large section on how to cope with the problems of being a stepfather. Ari spent many subsequent evenings reading the books.

After Bobby Kennedy's tragic death, Jackie finally agreed to accept Onassis' proposal of marriage. According to a story in a book published in Europe, Jackie telephoned Ari in Greece from New York, demanded that he marry her, and refused to take no for an answer; Ari, who had decided to rewed his divorced wife Tina, was stunned; but the next day Ari called his family together and announced, "I must marry Jacqueline. My decision is irrevocable."

Jackie's friends and relatives guffawed at the tale. Hugh Auchincloss, Jr., her half-brother, who lives on Park Avenue in New York City, rarely permits interviews on the subject of Ari and Jackie, but he scoffed at this particular wild yarn. "I don't believe any of it," he said. "It wouldn't be characteristic of either of them to act that way." Another close friend was equally brief but more to the point. "It's bullshit," he said.

On October 20, 1968, in a tiny chapel on the island of Skorpios, thirty-nine-year-old Jackie and sixty-two-year-old Ari* marched slowly around a simple altar three times, doing the dance of Isaiah—the traditional closing rite of the Greek Orthodox wedding ceremony —and were pronounced man and wife.

Within the hour, world opinion burst forth. Some of the comments are well-known. The classic was the headline in *Expressen,* a Stockholm newspaper: "JACKIE, HOW COULD YOU?" Less historic but equally trenchant was the one in the Long Island *Press:*

WHY DID JACKIE CHOOSE ONASSIS?
THERE ARE WELL OVER A BILLION REASONS

A columnist for *L'Espresso,* an Italian newspaper, fumed: "Onassis, a grizzled satrap with liver-colored skin, a fleshy nose, a wide horsy grin—that's the lady's new husband!" An editorial in *Bild-Zeitan,* a West

---

* Ari's passport listed his age as sixty-nine, but he explained this was because he'd had to lie about his age in order to get work in Argentina when he emigrated there from Greece as a sixteen-year-old.

German newspaper, asserted, "All the world is indignant."

Maria Callas, Onassis' longtime intimate companion, said, "She did well to give a grandfather to her children." And a foreign ambassador in Athens made a comment that bounced around the world and, presumably, did not enchant the Greek government or his own: "I am convinced that she married Onassis to secure the financing of John-John's presidential campaign in the year 2000. And besides, Onassis is the only man who can afford her."

But more fascinating than these were the observations made privately by world leaders and others of high rank. These juicy tidbits were passed along by American and foreign correspondents interviewed at the National Press Club in Washington:

• Richard M. Nixon, then a presidential candidate, to a member of his staff: "The dignity of the office [the presidency] has just suffered a severe blow."

• General Dwight D. Eisenhower, former president of the United States, to an aide: "Those Democrats will stoop to anything to get the Greek vote."

• Nikita S. Khrushchev, a former premier of the Soviet Union to a newsman who covered the blunt-speaking Russian: "I used to like the way she behaved, but the capitalist system makes you do horrible things. The whole Onassis marriage was done for profit."

• A Greek physician who once treated Onassis: "She knew that he was playing around with dictators, but it didn't bother her one bit. Jack and Robert would turn over in their graves if they knew. I say Jackie deserves Ari and vice versa!"

• François (Papa Doc) Duvalier, president of Haiti: "There is no accounting for the weird tastes of women."

• A man who had served as a cabinet member during the Kennedy administration: "The marriage is ridiculous, preposterous, ludicrous, absurd, grotesque, rococo, and positively stinks!"

CHAPTER II

A Matched Pair

Many Jackie-watchers around the world echoed the anger and perplexity about the wedding expressed by celebrated persons and newspaper headlines. "Why?" they wondered. How different they were! She the lovely Ariel; he the gnomelike Caliban. She the beautiful, sophisticated, fascinating former First Lady of the United States; he the crude, unattractive little man— he stood five feet five inches tall in his handmade shoes, and was thus two inches shorter than she. And he was, as a final bafflement, so much older than she.

The conclusion almost everyone quickly reached was that it was a classic case of opposites attracting. Yet Jackie and Ari, as we shall see, had a more harmonious relationship in the early years of their marriage than was generally believed, and it was a kind of harmony that could not have been achieved if the partners had brought discordant elements into their union.

Jackie and Ari were not as different as most people believe. They were certainly no more different than millions of other couples who are reasonably happy with one another—again, we emphasize, in the beginning years—and they shared a number of interests and behavioral characteristics. Not all were praiseworthy, to be sure, but that's not the point. What mattered was that common meeting grounds did exist, and because they did, Jackie and Ari understood and accepted one another.

Here are some of their more significant similarities.

To begin with, each possessed *an obsessive need to collect celebrities*. Even when Jackie was very young, she met many famous people. Shortly before her seventh birthday, her father introduced her to "America's funniest man—Fred Allen." Allen was followed by aviator Charles Lindbergh, the Duke of Windsor, and President Franklin Delano Roosevelt.

Her interest in people with "big names" has continued throughout her life. In 1951, when she was a student at George Washington University, she entered a contest sponsored by *Vogue* magazine. One of the things she had to do was to write an essay about "People I Wish I Had Known." Jackie selected Irish-born English playwright Oscar Wilde, French Romantic poet Charles Baudelaire, and Russian ballet producer Sergei Diaghilev. Jackie won the contest, defeating 1,280 other college girls.

Not many years later, Jackie no longer had to settle for an essay celebrity—she was meeting the real thing. A Kennedy aide who has known Jackie socially as well as professionally says, "She collects big names the way other people collect stamps. Her personal museum of the distinguished contains *hundreds* of black-and-magenta British Guianas." *

The Jackie Kennedy Onassis gallery of famous people has included Charles de Gaulle, Haile Selassie, Queen Elizabeth and Prince Philip, Pakistanian presi-

---

* The black-and-magenta British Guiana is a postage stamp reputed to be the rarest in the world and presently valued at $300,000.

dent Ayub Khan, Irish president Eamon de Valera
. . . a veritable *International Who's Who.*

Onassis, too, got a special thrill out of consorting
with celebrities, and he liked to refer to them as "bosom
buddies." Occasionally, he'd prove this close comrade-
ship by making an especially renowned female his bed
companion. His salons and yacht were constantly
filled with the world's best-known women and men.
Among the steady stream of guests were Princess Grace
and Prince Rainier, Greta Garbo, Elizabeth Taylor,
Princess Margaret and Lord Snowden, Cary Grant, Sir
Laurence Olivier, Aly Kahn, Dame Margot Fonteyn,
Humphrey Bogart, Gregory Peck, the Duchess of
Kent, Gary Cooper, Douglas Fairbanks, King Peter of
Yugoslavia, Bernard Baruch, and Princess Lee Radzi-
will.

Onassis' biggest social acquisition, however, was
Sir Winston Churchill, who was a frequent passenger
aboard the *Christina* on cruises in the Mediterranean,
the Canary Islands, and the Caribbean. Ari would go
to great lengths to insure continuation of the relationship—before each cruise, a messenger would deliver
to Churchill a list of proposed fellow passengers for
his approval.

An aide reports, "He [Ari] used to have long conversations with Winston about everything—history, the
classics, writing, philosophy, politics." Ari would
spend hours telling Jackie his Winston stories. Onassis
wept unashamedly at Churchill's funeral and considered him "the greatest man of our times—or possibly
all times!"

Sir Winston had repaid the compliment several
years before when he had said, "Undoubtedly Ari is
a genius, but why does he constantly have to hear
such adulation from people like me?"

Maria Callas understood this aspect of Ari's nature. "He is obsessed by famous women," she once said. "He was obsessed with me because I was famous. Now she [Jackie] and her sister, they have obsessed him, and they are even more famous."

Earl Blackwell, the distinguished international social arbiter, said, "Onassis was avid in his pursuit of the famous. He went far out of his way to seek the company of people who made news. He loved being photographed with celebrities, and quite early in his career learned a little trick with which all persons who seek publicity are familiar. When he saw that a photographer was preparing to take a picture, he would insinuate himself into the center, never standing at the end. He had learned that picture editors, because of space requirements, might crop out the end persons but could not eliminate the ones in the center."

Ari had always had *the need to be at stage center*, and Jackie appears to possess a similar need. "Off-stage, Jackie is usually quiet and shy," a longtime friend of Jackie's explained. "But whenever she gets to a large party, she immediately has to become the belle of the ball—it's almost as if it's mandatory. It's always been that way."

A woman who was Jackie's classmate at Miss Porter's School said, "At one very elaborate coming-out party, Jackie entered feeling lower than the proverbial snake; she'd been in a horse show earlier in the day and had failed to win a ribbon. Just before we were announced, Jackie pinched herself. Yes, I said 'pinched herself'! Suddenly, I could see a tremendous transformation come over her. Suddenly, she became radiant and alive. From that moment on, she was in constant demand with all the boys.

"She's still in great demand with all the men," the

woman went on. "I guess having Jackie on your invitation list guarantees a successful party, but I've heard some hostesses complain that it's too high a price to pay. I suppose I'm being catty, but most women worry because Jackie is such a big flirt. She's changed her routine slightly. Now, she puts on that Mona Lisa smile and looks serene. *Pow!* All the men flock around her. But I really don't think Jackie gives a damn about them."

Onassis would be moody and detached until he attended a cocktail or dinner party. Then he'd become the center of attraction. If he felt he wasn't receiving the attention due him, he'd resort to sure-fire, notice-getting devices. At one Paris party, he removed his jacket, tie, and shirt. Then he ordered the other men present to do the same. Soon, some of the women—including a popular American film star—also removed their tops.

At another party—this one aboard the *Christina*—he proposed that the winner of a particular game be allowed to caress all the female guests. Ari won, and guests reported he enjoyed his reward.

Even Onassis' employees knew their boss wouldn't tolerate second best. The unspoken rule always was that he was to be star attraction—wherever they went, whatever the occasion. Here's one case in point.

In September 1967, Earl Blackwell staged a party that *The Times* of London called "the greatest international ball of the century." It was given at the seventeenth-century Palazzo Rezzonico in Venice to raise money to restore the art works damaged by the disastrous floods in Florence. Guests included Elizabeth Taylor, Rose Kennedy, Princess Grace and Prince Rainier, Douglas Fairbanks, Jr., and scores of other glittering personalities. Clearly, it was an event at which Onassis had to shine.

Guests had been asked to appear in costume, and many went to considerable expense. Just before the event, the heavens opened and Venice was pelted with one of the heaviest downpours in years. The costly costumes were ruined, makeup ran, hairdos were a shambles.

The only way to reach the palazzo was by boat. If a guest had a large yacht, he would go to the party in a launch; others would come by water taxi. Minutes after the rain began, the boats were snarled in the worst sea-traffic jam in the city's history.

Ari, who had sailed to Venice aboard the *Christina,* had embarked in his white launch. His seamen, well-schooled, were determined not to allow the other craft to outmaneuver them to the dock. They pushed and bumped through the monstrous jam-up of boats, outraging other celebrities. Later, at the party, knots of guests expressed disgust at the way Onassis had bullied his way through the tie-up.

"The pull of the sea," wrote biographers Ann Pinchot and Gordon Langley Hall, "is one of the links that forged the chain of love for Jacqueline and her husband, John Kennedy." *The pull of the sea* did no less for Jackie and Ari.

From childhood, the sea held a deep fascination for Jackie. Often she would sit upon the shore with thick notepaper on her lap and compose verses that mirrored her feelings. As early as age ten, she composed a poem called "Sea Joy." And when she was fourteen, Jackie wrote a poem called "Sailing" that was printed in the *East Hampton* [New York] *Star.* It began: "I only care for the lovely sea."

A relative who frequently cruised on the *Christina* with Ari said, "How Ari loved the sea! You could see it on his face, in his every expression. His idea of paradise was when the *Christina* was far from land and was moving. It was always that way. When Ari was about seventeen or so—it was soon after he left for Argentina—he won a rowing contest and spent his prize, about three of your American dollars, on a secondhand telescope. He said he'd take that telescope with him every Sunday when he'd go to the harbor for relaxation. He'd sit and look out to sea, and, I guess, dream of the day he'd own part of it."

Jackie and Ari also each had a *strong temper*. One of Jackie's relatives says, "When people describe her, the terms they use most often are 'ladylike,' 'well-bred,' and 'cultured.' She is all of these. Nonetheless, this poised and polished woman can erupt like Vesuvius when provoked."

Once a servant accidentally spilled shoepolish on one of her expensive Paris creations. Jackie blew up. The shocked girl reddened, then burst into tears. But Jackie softened, gave the girl a lace handkerchief to staunch her tears, and told her to keep it.

Jackie has sometimes used colorful language at official gatherings. Once, when she was the First Lady, she was seated at dinner next to a very dour-looking foreign minister. Jackie supposedly said sweetly, "Why, you're not quite as much of a bastard as I'd heard you were!" The startled diplomat smiled weakly as he gulped his soup.

The former White House aide who reported the Gromyko story added, "Jackie speaks her mind, no matter what. She used that exact 'bastard routine' on several different people."

A maid who worked on Jackie's grandfather's estate

JACKIE AND ARI

in East Hampton says, "Even as a youngster she had a temper. She would carry on something awful until she got her way. Once, I remember, her father refused to allow her to go to a movie with some friends of her own age because he felt that ten-year-olds needed an adult chaperone. She jumped up and down, hollered real loud, and twisted her face into a thousand shapes. Her poor dad finally had to give in—she did that with everything."

"She was a pretty little thing," recalls a former employee of East Hampton's exclusive Maidstone Club. "But her temper belonged to a person five times her age and five times her size. If she was told that she would have to wait to get on the tennis court, or if swimming towels weren't given to her right away, she blew up."

That temper has remained with Jackie throughout her life. When her first husband was president, she redecorated the White House, and, for the most part, the results were excellent. In the family dining room, however, she installed some antique mid-nineteenth-century wallpaper depicting battle scenes from the American Revolution. The president commented that the scenes were so depressing that they gave him indigestion, and he asked Jackie to remove the wallpaper. Her reaction wasn't just negative. A White House servant says the former First Lady did everything but hurl the soup at the president.

(Betty Ford, the current First Lady, agreed with Kennedy and recently had the wallpaper taken off and the family room painted a bright yellow.)

The Onassis temper was equally well-known. Once he was proudly showing Churchill how the swimming pool on the *Christina* became an elaborate dance floor by the push of a button.

"He did this several times," says a crew member. "Then it got jammed midway. Onassis told the engineer to fix it immediately. But twenty minutes went by, and it was still stuck. That did it. He called the engineer and said, 'How many stripes on your cap?'

" 'Four, sir.'

" 'You know what you can do with those stripes?'

" 'What, sir?'

" 'Jam them down your fucking cap!'

"The conversation was in Greek and Churchill heard the word *skoufos*. He asked Onassis what it meant. He was told that it means cap.

" 'Cap?' Churchill shouted. 'Why are you telling him to fix it with a cap? Tell him to use a Goddamn screwdriver!' "

"Ari would swear, but it was very democratic," says an Olympic Airways employee. "He didn't discriminate —he swore at everybody. Once, when he was returning to Athens from London, he noticed that the 'F' on the neon sign that normally reads 'Fly Olympic' was out. Although it was three in the morning, he called the person he thought was responsible. Mr. Onassis could swear in six languages; this time he used Greek.

" 'Olympic never, never lies, you stupid son-of-a-bitch! Get your fucking ass over here and fix that fucking "F"!' "

One day, in the winter of 1974, Onassis arrived for an examination at the office of a world-famous cardiologist in New York. The doctor, whose patients include many distinguished persons, was occupied. When Onassis learned he could not be seen at once, he exploded into a temper tantrum, stomping and bellowing so loudly he could be heard all through the suite of offices.

Afterward, the doctor observed, "It was a cortisone rage." The drug, which Onassis was taking for myasthenia gravis, a disease characterized by abnormal fatigue and muscular weakness, can sometimes cause mental and emotional upheavals. Replied the nurse drily, "And when he's not on cortisone?"

Jackie and Ari were alike in other ways. Both were devoted to their children. Both were knowledgeable about the mores of the rich and famous, and accepted them—neither could be shocked by the intrigues, gossip, or casual sexual relationships within their social circle. Both knew the difficulties of making one's way in a hostile world. Both were intensely ambitious. Both were intellectually quick. And both loved people, laughter, friends, and the very best things the world can provide.

CHAPTER III

She

The daughter of rich, handsome John Vernou Bouvier III and the slender, beautiful Janet Lee, both of whom were socially prominent in the madcap era of F. Scott Fitzgerald, young Jacqueline Bouvier was brought up as a very rich little girl in New York and Southampton, deprived of nothing she wanted.

By the time she was five, she was a spoiled child and a large handful to her nurses and governesses, none of whom lasted long in the Bouviers' employ—largely because of Jackie's behavior. At exclusive Miss Chapin's School in New York, she was a horror to her teachers. (One of her biographers, Mary Van Rensselaer Thayer, puts it this way. "She was an outlaw. Her brightness, almost precocity, made school too easy. She finished studying before her classmates, and then found nothing but mischief to occupy her mind and energies.")

One day, Janet Bouvier was overseeing Jackie and a group of her little friends in Central Park. Jackie became ornery. Janet said to one of the children, "Isn't she a naughty little girl?"

She had hardly expected the blunt reply—"She's the very worst girl in school!" As Janet stared, Jackie's friend went on, "Jackie does something bad every day.

She gets sent to Miss Stringfellow's every day—well, almost every day."

The formidable Ethel Stringfellow, Miss Chapin's School's legendary headmistress, cowed most students. Not Jackie. When Janet wanted to know what happened at these sessions with the headmistress, her small daughter informed her, "She says a lot of things, but I don't listen."

Jack Bouvier and Janet were divorced in 1940; the case involved overtones of scandal. At first, Janet had sought the divorce in New York State, where, at the time, the only grounds for divorce were adultery. Later she went to Nevada, where the decree was eventually granted. Jackie and her sister became "visitation-rights" children, shuttling between parents.

The divorce, coming at a crucial time in Jackie's life, probably triggered a wide range of reactions —among them rage, hate, self-pity, and resentment, all of which are common in children whose protective shelter is abruptly removed. Jackie adored her handsome, dynamic father, the dark and dashing "Black Jack" Bouvier who maintained a deep year-round tan and cut such an impressive figure in the high social world of the times. (Bouvier's classmates at Yale had dubbed him "the sheik" as a tribute to his classy looks and unbelievable success with women.)

When her parents separated and her home life was shattered Jackie withdrew into a private world from which she never completely emerged. Worshipping her father, loving her mother, she was torn by conflicting loyalties that exacerbated her feelings of helplessness, guilt, anxiety, and insecurity. She was asked, in effect, to take sides, and this is an impossible choice for any child who loves *both* parents and needs their love in return.

Thus the extrovert who delighted in showing off before any audience, the gay, sparkling, mischievous companion, became all at once quiet, shy, and reserved. Only some of the changes in her personality could be attributed to the onset of puberty—her withdrawal was too extreme and too sudden for normal adolescent behavior. She smiled seldom, avoided all friends, spent her days walking alone or in a room staring at the walls and ceiling. "She passed her days in a dream-like trance," say her biographers, Pinchot and Hall. "She went through all the gestures expected of her at school, but most of her life was an inner one."

Years later Jackie's sister-in-law Ethel Kennedy observed, "You'll have a hard time getting to the bottom of *that* barrel." Ethel had sensed the existence of Jackie's private inner core. Few in Camelot knew how strongly her parents' divorce had affected twelve-year-old Jackie. The shock may have been as profound to her in some ways as the one her own children, especially Caroline, underwent when John Kennedy was slain.

Through the years, Jackie would emerge from the shadows of her own moods and then retreat again; she was rather like the sun slipping in and out of clouds. Sometimes her sunny self would shine for days at a time; other times the dark moods and the happy ones would alternate during the course of a single afternoon.

When the gloom descended—and nobody could predict when this would be—Jackie wouldn't emerge from her self-imposed seclusion no matter how urgent the reason. Surely a "request" from matriarch Rose Kennedy to any member of the family has to be considered a command, but, on several occasions, Jackie ignored Rose's invitations. Once, while she was visiting

Rose at the Kennedy winter home in Palm Beach, some important friends of the family arrived for lunch. Rose sent for Jackie, requesting she come down. Jackie, recuperating from the birth of her son, sent back word that she could not appear for lunch. Nor did she.

On other occasions, Rose, who knew how effective a wife could be in furthering her husband's political career, would suggest that Jackie appear at Washington functions, either by herself or with the president. Jackie did as she pleased, showing up when and where she wished.

Jackie has a special sense of style, a love of all things beautiful; she is the archetype of the real, knowing woman all other women secretly admire; she is fashion's empress; she is a girl-woman, still a sensuous nymphet with those large eyes, that child's smile, her teen-ager's figure. She is also one of the world's shrewdest women.

All this implies that Jackie Kennedy Onassis is a brittle person whose consuming interest is self. Not so. Central to her life is her devotion—not to herself, but to her two children. "I am a woman above everything else," she once said in a rare moment of self-revelation. "I love children and I think that seeing one's children grow up is the most delightful thing any woman can think about."

In her own way, on her own level, she will fight as fiercely to protect her children, Caroline and John, as any mother. Throughout the years since the assassination of the president, she has been a lioness when it comes to her offspring, surrounding them with an impregnable wall of privacy that has consisted of Secret Service men as a first line of defense, and has included phalanxes of nurses, governesses, secretaries, and other aides to back them up. Once Mrs. Auchincloss and Lee Radziwill suggested to Jackie that she recognize the intense world interest in the children and hold a once-yearly press conference at which the children might answer questions before they retreated once again behind the unscalable wall. Jackie didn't need even a moment to weigh the proposal. She replied at once: "Absolutely not!"

It was Jackie's determination to protect what she called her "emotional privacy" that impelled her to bring suit in 1966 to block publication in *Look* Magazine of the serialization of the William Manchester book, *Death of a President*. She demanded that the publishers remove or modify several passages —among them, one relating that she had been unable to make a decision on how to tell Caroline that her father had been killed; an account in her own words of the night she had spent with the president before he was slain; and quotations from a love letter she had written to John Kennedy. She would not be swayed; her children's privacy and her own were inviolate and inviolable. And she won her fight. *Look* agreed to remove or modify the passages.

Few Americans are aware that Jackie had previously threatened to resort to the courts to guard her children's privacy. Another book was involved— Maude Shaw's *White House Nanny*. Miss Shaw, an Englishwoman, had been the Kennedy children's nurse for seven years and had been with them when news of the assassination came.

Jackie hadn't wanted Maude to write the book in the first place. "It would make capital of the children," she had told her. But the book was written anyway, and an English publisher made plans to release it.

Word reached Jackie, who asked Sol M. Linowitz, a friend who was an official at Xerox Corporation, to help her prevent publication.

Linowitz called the publisher, Michael Borissow, who flew to New York in September 1965 and conferred with Mr. Linowitz, Pamela Turnure (Mrs. Kennedy's secretary), and a representative of the attorney general at the Hotel Pierre. The conferees agreed that some one hundred words, dealing with how the children were informed of the slaying of their father, would be eliminated from the manuscript. Mr. Borissow said later that the deletions covered items Jackie considered "a little too personal," and disclosed that there had been "some threat of injunction" against publication if the matter was not resolved.

In 1968, Jackie became enraged once again when she felt her privacy had been breached. She fired her family cook, pretty young Annemarie Huste, who had worked for her for two years, because she felt the twenty-four-year-old German girl was exploiting the family name. Miss Huste had been interviewed in a New York newspaper and some of her recipes had appeared in a magazine.

The action was not untypical, for Jackie is a demanding employer. "She maintains a suitable distance between herself and her servants and employees," said Pearl Buck in *The Kennedy Women*. For their part, the help come to her awed and excited, but soon lose their reverence, and the excitement diminishes markedly as the work piles up and the pay remains small. Through the years, they have never referred to Jackie by name; it has always been "she." One former member of the household says, "I loved the children. They were wonderful, unspoiled, and generous kids. But *she* was a terror."

CHAPTER IV

He

"On the one hand, Onassis could discuss Greek mythology with the sureness and delicacy of a learned college professor," a business competitor once said. "And a minute later, he could be the crudest peasant. The man was a true riddle."

The guessing game of "choose the real Onassis" got its impetus in the summer of 1923, when sixteen-year-old Ari emigrated to Buenos Aires. He made the crossing in the twelve thousand-ton *Tommaso di Savoia,* and the transatlantic trip for most of the voyagers was far from pleasant. The five-hundred-fifty-foot vessel, which could accommodate six hundred passengers, was packed with more than four times that number. Refugees jammed her holds, stacked three high in bunks— there were so many that the ship's galley could feed them only one meal a day.

Young Ari, however, who had paid eighty dollars for his trip, bribed the purser with a five-dollar bill to let him bed down in an unused enclosure in the ship's aft, away from the foul stench of the steerage, where, if there was room to stand at all, the passengers would slip and slide on the excrement or vomit.

Aristotle Socrates Onassis, whose bankroll was now sixty dollars, thus sailed comfortably down the South

Atlantic to start a new life in Argentina. He walked down the gangplank on September 21, 1923 into a strange new land where he knew nobody and had no citizenship.

Six years later, he was a millionaire importer of tobacco.

It was a Horatio Alger-like rise, although it was managed by tactics Alger would hardly have recommended. In later years, during relaxed moments when the ouzo flowed freely, Onassis would relate with relish some of the tricks he devised to help him accumulate his first million.

At the bar of the King George Hotel in Constitution Square, the center of modern Athens, an Onassis cousin,* a short, thin man in his late fifties who worked for ten years for one of Onassis' European offices, talked for an afternoon about the tycoon. He knew Ari intimately; he had spent many hours with him at his homes—drinking with him, listening to him tell stories of his youth, his adventures, and his ambitions.

"When Ari drank a lot," the cousin said, "out would come the stories. He was full of them. He could make a timetable sound exciting! I could listen to him for hours. He'd slam his fist on the table when he came to a part he felt was important. One time he slammed the table so hard he broke it, and also his fist!

"He told me: 'You are allowed to do anything in business to succeed. Anything! Once I spread the word that a competitor's tobacco was full of germs that gave out a strange disease. Not only did the man lose a sale, but he also lost his tobacco when the health depart-

---

* Onassis employed many relatives. When he died, there were more than fifty on the payroll.

ment wanted to condemn it.' Then Ari laughed and laughed."

Onassis was a refugee of war. He had fled from the onslaught of the Turkish forces under Mustafa Kemal Ataturk, the founder of modern Turkey who, in that blazing summer of 1923, had sacked Ari's birthplace, the city of Smyrna (now renamed Izmir) on the Aegean Sea. One of the richest and largest cities of Asia Minor, Smyrna had been ruled by the Ottoman Turks until 1919; then it had been captured by the Greeks. Onassis' father, Socrates Onassis, had settled there in the 1880s, and had married a beautiful eighteen-year-old girl, Penelope Dologlu,* and developed a prosperous business as a tobacco merchant.

On January 20, 1906, Aristotle was born, and the mystery that has followed him for the next seven decades seems to have begun almost at once. His Argentine passport, which he acquired later, puts his birth date at 1900, but Onassis was to explain that he had deliberately falsified his age to enable him to find employment. The true date, he insisted, was 1906. We tried to locate the exact date, but were told that birth records had been destroyed when the Turks burned and pillaged the city.

Onassis grew up in troubled times. The ancient city where he lived, which had been a Greek colony two thousand years before, was captured by Greek troops when he was thirteen and annexed once again to the mother country. The Turks smoldered, and, in 1922, Ataturk and his Turkish nationalists launched an offensive that culminated in the destruction of Smyrna. A million Greeks perished; countless others were stripped of all they owned and were deported. The invaders

---

* She died at the age of twenty-six, and Socrates Onassis remarried.

executed Ari's Uncle Alexander; Uncles John and Basil were placed in internment camps, as were his stepmother and half-sisters; his father was put in jail in Smyrna. Ari and his grandmother were the only ones remaining at home.

Ari never forgave the Turks for these injustices, and his hate for them was apparent throughout his life. He always insisted that a dollar didn't know its owner; yet on more than one occasion he sold cargoes of oil to countries other than Turkey, even though he could have made considerably more if Turkey had been the customer.

Ari once had a memorable conversation with a high Turkish official who constantly made reference to his distinguished background. The meeting took place at London's Hotel Claridge, where Onassis maintained a permanent suite. At the outset, Ari was most reasonable and gentlemanly.

Onassis:	You speak many languages, don't you?
Visitor:	I have the privilege of being able to discourse in French, English, Greek, Italian, Spanish, and of course, Turkish.
Onassis:	"Well, then, I'll say my piece in all those languages so you will be sure to understand my message:
(Greek)	*Ise enas apateonas pseftes gamimenos poutsos!*
(Turkish)	*Sahtekar yalancinin birisin!*
(Spanish)	*Usted es un enredador mentiroso singado pinga!*

Rapid-fire, he spoke next in French and Italian,

and finally concluded in English, "You are a crooked, lying, fucking prick!"

Ari's father insisted that his young son flee the country before the Turks could arrest him. On Ari's final visit to his father in prison, he passed him food, cigarettes, and money through the bars. Then the two kissed solemnly and Socrates told his son, "Onassis is a proud name—always remember to be faithful to it!" *

(With the help of the U.S. vice-consul, John L. Parker, Socrates Onassis was eventually freed, but by that time his young son had bowed to his urgent plea to leave the fallen city.)

Disguised as a U.S. seaman in a baggy uniform Parker had found for him, Ari sailed from the city of Smyrna in an American destroyer. On September 3, he stepped aboard the *Tommaso di Savoia* for the long voyage to Argentina. He was a boy without a country—his Turkish citizenship had been revoked; in his pocket was a document issued by the League of Nations describing him as a stateless person.

Onassis soon found a job in a Buenos Aires telephone company. Initially, he worked as a laborer; then he got a job as a mechanic, and he finally rose to executive status. At first, the pay wasn't very good (he averaged twenty-five cents an hour), but there were agreeable fringe benefits: dozens of pretty girls were employed as operators at the telephone company. Ari dated a different one each week; he'd take her out rowing and then grade her meticulously—looks, re-

---

* Another version of the story is that Ari's father criticized the youth for paying too high a bribe to get the family out of jail. A resentful Ari immediately left the country. Onassis, however, constantly gave out the first explanation. It certainly is more romantic.

ceptivity, dress, love of the sea, and so on. One attractive young lady who received very high marks in most categories got a D in "love of parents."

By 1926, Ari hadn't singled out a steady girlfriend, but he *had* accumulated a small fortune—it should be noted that there were no income tax laws in Argentina —and before he was twenty-four he had been named Greek vice-consul general. In his official post, he supervised arrivals and departures of grain vessels from Greek ports, and in this position he was able to make a momentous discovery—shipping companies, suffering huge losses in the Great Depression, were abandoning their freighters in ports around the world. Ari found six Canadian vessels riding at anchor, bid for them, and successfully picked up twelve million dollars' worth of shipping for one hundred-twenty thousand dollars—1 percent of their cost.

So began a career unique in world history. The squat, dark-eyed boy who had walked virtually penniless from the crowded refugee ship was to become a legend before he turned fifty. He amassed a fortune variously estimated at five hundred million dollars to one billion dollars, owned lavish homes and apartments on three continents, controlled more than one hundred ships (each of which was worth many millions), lived like a medieval lord on his own private island estate in the Ionian Sea, sailed the seas aboard a luxury yacht, made love to some of the world's most beautiful and talented women, ran an international airline, owned the casino at Monte Carlo in Monaco, took on governments in conflicts over oil and fishing, talked daily to the most influential men on the globe (including heads of state), wed the daughter of the man who was then the richest in Greece, lived openly with one of the world's best-known opera stars, and married the widow of a president of the United States.

Ari's cousin once asked him his formula for success. Onassis thought a moment and came up with this five-point program:

1. Work twenty hours a day.
2. Be willing to take risks.
3. Lend an ear to "important" gossip.
4. Offer tempting bait.
5. Don't wait too long for triumphs; if they don't happen soon enough, start "goosing" them along.

He used the five rules to amass his fleet, which was larger than most countries' navies and employed more than three thousand men. In general, the vessels belonged to a separate corporation registered in Panama and flew the Liberian flag.

Despite the size of his vast armada, Ari was personally aware of the exact location of each ship. When the Suez Canal was shut in 1967 and the longer route around the Cape became necessary, Onassis juggled his ships continuously, because he realized that the closing of the canal made tanker space scarce and that oil merchants were prepared to pay accordingly. As usual, he guessed right, and his earnings increased tremendously. At the time he said, "Wars can make you rich if you play your cards right."

In the early 1950s, civil and criminal suits were filed against him by the U.S. Justice Department; these involved surplus ships that he had bought. Under the law, the surplus vessels could be purchased only by U.S. corporations. He was charged with falsely representing that the ships would remain in American hands by establishing dummy corporations in the United States so that he could purchase the ships. After years of negotiations, the U.S. government, which had filed a twenty-million-dollar suit against him, finally settled the civil suit for seven million dollars and dropped the criminal charges.

Ari was always looking for profitable challenges. He believed that he could restore Monte Carlo to its former glory, and in 1952 he invested one and a half million dollars in 52 per cent of the stock of Monaco's Societé des Bains de Mer, which included the casino (where he never gambled), the yacht club, the Hotel de Paris, and about one-third of Monaco's three hundred seventy-five acres. At the time, Prince Rainier thought it was a "good deal," and both he and Onassis worked together to restore the famed resort to the status it had once had.

A few years later, however, Rainier had changed his mind. "I was taken for a sucker," he said. "All Onassis was interested in was quick money-making projects!" Ari felt that he, too, had been "gypped" and had paid an exorbitant price. Eventually, he sold out completely and said he suffered a loss, which prompted him to issue another maxim: "When you make a mistake, admit it and get out fast!"

Before Onassis' will was made known, Greek newspapers carried stories about how quickly he would be forgotten because he had contributed nothing of value to his country. Professor John Georgakis, of Athens, who had been a close associate of Onassis and has served in many government posts, disagreed. "If nothing else," said the distinguished professor of law, "Ari's creation of Olympic Airways will always be a towering monument to his ingenuity. He gave birth to the airline, saw that it operated smoothly, and turned it into a formidable international carrier."

And a former employee said, "Ari could have made more profits from tankers, but he chose Olympic out of sheer patriotism . . . and besides, Jackie got free transportation."

Whatever the reason behind Olympic Airways' formation, it was obvious that Onassis liked the idea of being the only person in the world to own a major international airline, and he could be quite aggressive when it came to acquiring potential customers. Once, at a party in New York's posh El Morocco, a couple said that they planned on taking a holiday in Europe; Ari quickly made certain that their carrier would be Olympic.

Onassis started Olympic Airways in 1957, when he bought three small airlines, and molded the company into a giant operation. He added new equipment and turned his first profit in 1963. Then, by threatening to pull out of the airline, he maneuvered the government into extending Olympic's monopoly status in Greece until 1966, and won a tax holiday until 1969. Just before his death, he sold Olympic to the Greek government—his estate will soon receive sixty-eight million dollars from the sale.

It is said that the Greek multimillionaire may have been gifted with some form of extrasensory perception that he harnessed for business. Ari may have possessed, at least in some measure, the mysterious ability of the human mind to see and know things without the use of any of the senses. (Many hundreds of laboratory tests have documented the existence of ESP—that certain persons possess the strange ability to "see" and "know" what others do not.)

The source of this information is a man who was associated with Onassis in many of his dealings during and after 1955. He is Nigel Neilson, Ari's personal liaison man in Great Britain and a close friend. Just one measure of the intimacy of their relationship:

Often Neilson would be awakened in the middle of the night by a telephone call. "Nigel," the familiar voice * would ask, "What time is it there?" Neilson, his eyes heavy-lidded, would glance at his watch. "It's 3 A.M." Ari, calling from the other end of the world, would express astonishment. He didn't realize. A brief apology, and he would launch into a lengthy discussion of an impending business transaction. "Ari could get by on three or four hours' sleep himself," Neilson says, "and he thought everybody lived that way."

Neilson works in a magnificent suite of offices at 24 Bruton Place in London's exclusive Mayfair section. He is chairman of the Neilson McCarthy Group, an international consultancy firm with offices in Australia, Malaysia, New Zealand, Singapore, and New York. He is fifty-five years old, a superb dresser, and has a cultivated voice not unlike that of Sir Laurence Olivier. This is perhaps not surprising, for Neilson studied at the Royal Academy of Dramatic Art and as a young man appeared on the London stage. Even today, he looks as though he could step into the role of an affable, successful executive in a West End comedy.

He said: "I remember clearly when our relationship began. I was asked if I would represent one of the largest shippers in the world. At first, I wasn't told who that was, but I soon discovered it was Onassis.

---

* Onassis' voice has always been described as possessing a buzz-saw quality—not true. After listening to him on tape, we'd say that his voice was firm but soft, and actually quite musical.

I had never met the man but I had heard a great deal about him and hadn't liked what I'd heard.

"I was told he wanted to see me in his Monte Carlo office. I flew there mostly out of curiosity. He looked up as I entered his office and said: 'What do the British think of me?'

"Before I could reply, he answered, 'They think I'm a Greek shit.'

"That did it. He won me over at once. . . .

"Ari had some special ability to foretell the future. Call it ESP. Many times, his top aides would advise him against making a particular deal—but he would disagree, enter into it, and it would work out extremely well. He knew something, he *saw* something, none of them did. It happened too many times to be coincidental.

"It was uncanny."

A number of Onassis' aides and business rivals offered evidence that appears to corrobate the existence of this strange trait.

At the National Yacht Club near Athens, one of the most exclusive in Greece, a partner in one of Greece's largest shipping firms (an organization not affiliated with the Onassis empire) related a conversation he had had with Ari in 1966.

"Olympic Airlines was losing money, and Ari was obviously concerned. I told him, 'Why don't you stick to ships, which you know about, instead of airplanes, in which you're not so expert?'

"Ari was silent for several minutes. Then he told me, 'I had a dream not long ago, a dream that Olympic was going to show a profit once we start flying across the ocean.'"

Until then, the airline had only serviced cities in Europe and the Middle East. When Ari implemented

49

the dream and turned Olympic into an international carrier, it began to show a profit.

And a *Christina* crew member says, "Onassis got messages—I don't know from where, but he got them all the time." This man adds that Sir Winston Churchill was given firsthand evidence of Ari's apparently unusual abilities.

The *Christina* employed a full-time telephone operator for ship-to-shore communications; he sat at a switchboard that plugged into forty phones. Calls from all over the world came to Onassis constantly. On numerous occasions while the former British prime minister was visiting abroad the yacht, a steward approached to tell Ari he was wanted on the phone. Each time, Ari would say with complete conviction, "I know who that is."

The *Christina* crewman says, "He would say the name, and most of the time he would be right, even though it was a person from far away, a person he hadn't heard from for a very long time."

Once Churchill asked in astonishment, "How in the world do you know?" Ari's reply, according to the crewman: "I don't know. I just do."

Perhaps the most powerful "premonition" of all was his feeling that he would marry the widow of President Kennedy. A cousin of Onassis told us, "As far back as 1966, two years before the wedding happened, he knew he would. He was positively sure."

Of course, whether or not an individual actually possesses extrasensory perception must be determined by careful laboratory experiments, and, to our knowledge, Onassis never underwent any of these tests. The evidence that he may have had some special awareness of something outside of himself is only anecdotal and surely would not persuade scientific investigators.

We are not, therefore, offering any "proof" that he was indeed gifted with ESP. But we do think that some of the tantalizing incidents we've mentioned might interest parapsychologists. Could it be that this phenomenon, now so widely discussed, was responsible, at least in some part, for the amassing of one of the world's greatest fortunes?

Ari's Midas touch and amatory conquests have always intrigued caricaturists. His dark glasses, short stature, aquiline nose, and toothy grin helped produce some hilarious cartoons in the international press. And yet the man whom the world considered so rich and powerful could be pathetically lonely at times. He would sit by himself for hours, or, restlessly, he would prowl around the *Christina* seeking out crew members and chatting with them. He would go ashore to spend several hours at Nikos' taverna. Or he would call his cousin and play games with him to fill an evening.

Once he telephoned the cousin and said, "I'll bet I know how to get to more out-of-the-way streets in Athens than you do!" Athens, which sprawls over a plain between the sea and the mountains, now has spread out to meet the port of Pireaus. The modern districts are simple enough to know; the older ones are an incomprehensible maze, even to Athenians.

The wager was a bottle of ouzo. Within minutes, Ari showed up at the cousin's house with his car and chauffeur. First Ari would name a street, and the cousin would have to tell the chauffeur where to go; then it would be Ari's turn to do the locating. After two hours of wandering through narrow alleys and around the fringes of the city, the cousin finally gave up. He could think of no more streets. Ari triumphantly named several more, collected his ouzo, and rode home.

He was not known for his philanthropy while he was alive; yet he was considered a soft touch. Strangers would stop him in Omonia Square, the large traffic-jammed popular heart of Athens, or in the Plaka, the old quarter where he loved to visit the taverns, and relate hard luck stories as their tears flowed. Ari would invariably stuff a roll of drachmas into their hands.

In 1972, two relatives of Jackie's made headlines when officials threatened to evict them from their sprawling home on Apoquogue Road in East Hampton after pronouncing it a health menace. Edith Bouvier Beale, who was seventy-seven, lived there with her daughter, fifty-four-year-old Edith Beale, surrounded by countless cats and empty cat-food boxes, the place a shambles. Jackie and her sister, Lee, contributed thirty thousand dollars to refurbish the place. Their contribution was publicized. Not revealed was that Ari also contributed fifty thousand dollars.

Ari was inconsistent in his generosity, however. Sometimes he would tip waiters well, other times poorly.

He was a prodigious worker, often spending twenty-four hours at his desk, sleeping a couple of hours,* then going through another equally hard day. Despite his far-flung business interests, he kept few personal records. His office was in his hat; he carried only a small notebook in which he jotted the barest essentials of his dealings. But he could usually remember every facet of every deal he made; he stored the details in his computerlike brain.

---

* He once said, "Don't sleep too much. If you sleep three hours less each night for a year, you will have an extra month and a half to succeed in."

His food tastes were simple. Whenever he arrived in New York, "21," the famed celebrity hangout, would reserve a corner table for him on the first-floor dining room. Sheldon Tannen, one of the owners, says, "He would arrive promptly at 1:15. No matter how cold it was, he would never wear an overcoat. He would walk in, hands in his pants pockets, always in a dark gray suit.

"On the table, we would place before him a plate of Parmesan cheese that had been broken with a fork, not cut with a knife; he preferred it that way. There would be slices of Bermuda onion and round slices of Kosher dill pickle, of which he was extraordinarily fond. There would also be a bottle of vodka set in ice, a small pitcher of tomato juice, quarters of lime, and a pitcher of water. He would then mix his own drinks."

A shrimp cocktail, a rare steak sandwich, chocolate macaroons, espresso coffee served in a large cup, and brandy would follow.

Only once did the menu vary. In 1972, the restaurant was hit by a strike. Ari crossed the picket line and sat at his usual table. The owners, manning the kitchen, were serving only two dishes—knockwurst and hamburgers. The patrons, all regulars, were dashing in and out of the kitchen, serving one another.

Socialite Liz Whitney was present with a party of ten. When she saw Onassis, she rushed into the kitchen and emerged with a hamburger that she set before him with a wide grin. Onassis looked up, astonished. "I never thought I'd live to see the day when I would be waited on by a Whitney," he said.

"When Ari wanted to turn on the charm, he could put Cary Grant and David Niven to shame," says one admiring woman who was exposed to the candlepower of his allure.

Even before he acquired his great wealth, females seemed to flock to Ari. He said that his first sexual experiences occurred when, as a teenager, he was seduced by a teacher.* This episode was followed by dozens of other sexual relationships. Ari was described as being "earthy, horny, romantic, and usually ready."

The landlady of his boardinghouse in Buenos Aires was so enamoured of him that he said he had to sneak out to avoid sleeping with her. The middle-aged wife of one of his employers in Argentina was another of his admirers. When he transferred to the night shift, Ari visited this woman in the morning, and one day the lady's husband came home unexpectedly. Ari managed to escape undetected, but in his haste, he left his tie in the bedroom. A few days later, the husband came to work wearing the tie.

Ari would shake his head sadly as he recalled the incident. "I suppose love isn't free," he'd say. "Even if you think so."

In 1934, Ari sailed from Buenos Aires to Genoa on a routine business trip. The first day out, he met Ingeborg Dedichen, a lovely thirty-three-year-old Norwegian divorcee who spent part of the night telling a sympathetic Onassis all about the breakup of her marriage. She also told him that her father, Thor Dahl, was the leading whaling shipper in all of Scandinavia.

When they landed, Ari decided to rent a house in Paris for the blonde Ingeborg. He visited her frequently and contributed to her support for many years. He once told an accountant, "She's worth every penny."

---

* We heard the same story many times, but Ari's age varied— thirteen, fourteen, fifteen, sixteen. In one version, the teacher liked the boy's lovemaking so much that she recommended him to other instructors.

"It was love at first sight," says Ingeborg in her book, *Onassis My Love,* published in France. "But Ari's love was often brutal. . . . He'd excuse himself by telling me, 'All self-respecting Greeks who love their wives beat them.' "

Discussing Ari's sexual adventures, Ingeborg writes, "Our first time together he told me of his past adventures with women—and they were many. However, Ari did not consider himself a sexual athlete. . . . He was fearless, cool, and level-headed. He demanded military obedience. His orders had to be carried out to the letter and acted upon instantly." She claims their close liaison came to an end when he met Tina Livanos.

Onassis was a carefree bachelor of thirty-nine when he decided the time had come for him to get married. He chose seventeen-year-old Athena (Tina) Livanos as his bride-to-be. The beautiful young girl was willing, but her father, Stavros Livanos, one of Greece's most powerful shipping tycoons, didn't approve of the union. Greek tradition required that older daughters be married before their sisters could wed, and Tina's sister, Eugenia, was two years her senior—and unmarried.

Ari was persistent, and he tried many schemes to get Papa Livanos to change his mind. He sent him expensive boxes of cigars wrapped in red, heart-shaped boxes that bore the inscription A.O./A.L. He sent dozens and dozens of long-stemmed roses to Mrs. Livanos, enclosing a card that said, "I'm sorry that these flowers aren't as pretty as you and your daughter."

When Ari learned that the Livanos family was spending some time at their summer home in Oyster Bay, Long Island, he painted the letters T.I.L.Y. on a flag, hoisted it aboard a speedboat, and crisscrossed past the Livanos waterfront home for hours. Later he explained to a puzzled Tina that the letters meant "Tina, I love you."

Livanos finally gave the persevering suitor permission to marry his daughter. On December 28, 1946, the marriage took place. The couple went on a two-month honeymoon aboard a lavishly equipped houseboat; they made a leisurely cruise of the Florida Keys. Then they traveled to Buenos Aires, where Ari proudly showed his bride the city.

Ari was so pleased with wedlock that he urged all his bachelor companions to try matrimony. A friend told us, "He'd bring you home unannounced and stare lovingly at a slightly peeved and embarrassed Tina. Then he'd say, 'Is there anything better that a man can have? I tell you, I'm the luckiest man in the world!' Then he would kiss her passionately."

At first, the marriage was ideal, but in 1959, Tina sued for divorce. She had given Onassis a son and heir, Alexander, and a daughter, Christina. Originally the suit, filed in New York State, charged that Onassis had committed adultery. Later Tina dropped the proceedings and was granted an uncontested divorce in 1960 in Alabama. There was considerable speculation in the world press that Onassis' relationship with diva Maria Callas had been the prime cause of the breakup.

Ari had always been passionate and tempestuous with women. His name had been linked with many great beauties, but his romances had been of short duration; he had always returned home to Tina and the children. The Callas affair, however, was different —Ari lived openly with the world-renowned singer and seemed to flaunt critics deliberately.

A *Christina* crew member said, "It start right on ship when he give big cruise for lots people. Mrs.

Onassis there too. She know everything. All guests know everything."

The guests on the cruise in question included Maria and her husband, Giovanni Meneghini, Sir Winston and Lady Churchill, Fiat president Umberto Agnelli and his wife Antonella, and assorted continental blue-bloods.

A saddened and angry Meneghini tells what happened. "The sea was choppy. I was ill. My wife was in one of her morose, taciturn moods, more like a tigress than ever. Onassis, on the other hand, was transformed. As the sea grew rougher, he became a real seadog, giving orders right and left. One night my wife returned from a party at the Istanbul Hilton and said she loved another man. After an hour, she admitted that the man was Aristotle Onassis."

When Ari was asked about Meneghini's charges, he smiled and said, "Friends have described me as a sailor, and sailors don't usually go for sopranos, but I would be flattered to have a woman of her class fall for me."

For the next ten years, the soprano showed that she had indeed fallen for the sailor; and although he privately loathed opera, the sailor was obviously fascinated by the dark-haired, tempestuous woman who had won worldwide acclaim. Says a friend who knew them both well: "They played together, laughed together, and shared almost everything together. Then Jackie came along!"

Now it was Maria's turn to be sad and angry. "He's obsessed by famous women. He was obsessed with me because I was famous. Jackie is even more famous. . . . First I lost my weight. Then I lost my voice, and now I've lost Onassis!"

CHAPTER V

Ari's Party

It is curious that Jackie and Ari met for the first time eight years earlier than either remembers.

Each has said that their initial meeting occurred in 1959 aboard the *Christina,* which was anchored at the time in the placid Mediterranean off Monte Carlo.

Neither could recall that, in 1951, the still youthful, dark-haired Onassis knelt on the parquet floor of a mansion in a Washington suburb and helped a maid pick up a trayful of canapés while twenty-two-year-old Jacqueline Bouvier, fresh from Vassar and the Sorbonne but not yet the Inquiring Camera Girl on the Washington *Times-Herald,* watched, her lovely face crinkled into a disapproving frown.

She had come to a cocktail party at the home of a reigning capital hostess on the arm of John Kennedy, then a rising young congressman from the 11th District of East Boston. Jack and Jackie were not yet married—he was to introduce her to his mother the following summer, and they were to wed on September 12, 1953.

The hostess of that party in 1951, a slender brunette, recalled the incident.

"I particularly remember it because of what happened," she said. "I saw Jacqueline talking in a group. Nearby was Aristotle Onassis. I weaved through the crowd, which had already filled the room to overflowing, and took Ari by the arm, turned him around, and told him there was someone I wanted him to meet. Then I introduced him to Jackie.

"But, horrors! As they were talking, one of the maids who was offering canapés was bumped by a guest, and the whole tray was overturned. Most of the canapés went on the floor, but some mayonnaise got on Jackie's shoe, and I could see that she was annoyed. Ari was marvelous. He helped the poor maid scoop up the mess."

Strange that both Jackie and Ari should forget their initial meeting.

Yet when one considers their personalities, perhaps it isn't quite so strange after all. Earlier it was pointed out that each was a collector of celebrities. Jackie, although fresh-faced and youthfully attractive, was not yet a great, acclaimed, much-desired beauty. And Ari, although already many times a millionaire, had yet to buy the bank at Monte Carlo and gain world celebrity.

Neither, in short, was the kind of person the other would seek out. And so, after the incident of the overturned canapé tray and a few more moments of conversation, each turned away and forgot the other.

The meeting they both remember occurred when Kennedy (then a senator from Massachusetts) and Jackie were visiting Kennedy's father, who had rented a villa on the Riviera. Tina, planning a party aboard the *Christina,* consulted with Ari about the guest list. It had to be special, because Winston Churchill would be present. Onassis, aware that young Kennedy held the wartime prime minister in high esteem, asked her to invite him.

Aboard ship, the handsome young couple was introduced to Sir Winston, who, knowing the senator was a strong presidential possibility in the 1960 elections, asked him what he thought of his chances of winning the nomination .

Kennedy told him, "I'm Catholic, you know."

"If that's your only difficulty," replied Churchill, "you can always change your religion and still be a good Christian."

Jack laughed and the two men continued talking politics while Ari showed Jackie about the opulent yacht. Enormously impressed, she later told a friend, "It's unbelievable . . . like an enchanted floating palace . . . the whole thing is right out of the *Arabian Nights!"*

Over the years, Jackie and Ari met several times at large soirees and exchanged chitchat. Usually, the *Christina* entered the conversation.

"Jackie had this strange thing about that boat," a former Kennedy servant said. "Every time she'd see a picture of another yacht she'd say, 'It doesn't compare to Onassis'.' I must have heard her say that at least a dozen times."

In 1961, the paths of Jackie and Ari crossed once again. With Lee and her husband, Prince Radziwill, and two Secret Service men, Jackie arrived in Greece for a five-day visit. They were entertained at the luxurious villa of another wealthy Greek shipowner, Markos Nomikos. On the second day, Ari popped up. He said he'd stopped by to pay his respects to "my good friend, Lee."

Ari then invited Jackie on a cruise, but two years were to elapse before she could accept.

Another Kennedy tragedy helped bring it about. Jackie was in Hyannisport, expecting her third baby. On August 7, 1963, a humid Wednesday, she took a drive with a Secret Service man and her two children, and then she suddenly felt ill. Dr. John Walsh, her obstetrician, who was vacationing on Cape Cod, was called. He ordered Jackie to fly to Otis Air Force Base in Falmouth, where a four-room suite had been made ready. Shortly after noon that day, after a swift trip by helicopter, Jackie gave birth five weeks prematurely to a four-pound, ten-ounce boy. Kennedy reached the hospital shortly afterward.

But the president's new son lived less than forty hours; the baby died a victim of hyaline membrane disease, a respiratory ailment that is responsible for the deaths of more premature infants than any other cause. None of the experts at Boston Children's Hospital Medical Center, where the baby was rushed, could save the boy.

Jackie remained at the cape, emotionally drained, speaking to nobody outside the family. She could barely summon up strength to telephone her sister, who was in Greece.

Lee, weeping, hung up the phone and told Ari about the tragedy. Immediately he offered to put the *Christina* at Jackie's disposal for her recuperation, for as long as she wished.

Although President Kennedy had qualms about his wife accepting the hospitality of a man who had been indicted for fraudulently dealing in surplus American Liberty ships, he assented because he felt the trip might help the First Lady snap out of her melancholy.

Evidently, the sea air was just what she needed, for shortly after the cruise began, Jackie threw a large shipboard dinner party and dance for eleven guests. Among them were the Radziwills, Ari's sister Artemis, and Under-Secretary of Commerce Franklin D. Roosevelt, Jr., who had been sent along to act as a chaperone.

Huge quantities of supplies were taken aboard the

Christina for Jackie's cruise—these included black figs, caviar, pomegranates, fresh strawberries, and cases of champagne. Ten extra seamen were added to the *Christina's* usual complement of fifty crew members for the special occasion, and a dance band, two hairdressers and a Swedish masseur were also employed.

Ari kept out of sight during the early part of Jackie's cruise aboard the *Christina,* emerging only when the yacht was nearing Lesbos, one of the legendary islands in the Aegean Sea near the coast of Turkey. He was a charming guide, and he took Jackie ashore and astonished her with his encyclopedic knowledge of Greek history. He showed her the beautiful mosques on the island, relating their histories; he pointed out the old town walls and discoursed about the distinguished poets and musicians born on the island; he pointed out the Leucadian rock from which the poet Sappho, according to legend, flung herself into the sea for the love of Phaon. Jackie was entranced.

The *Christina* sailed on to Crete, where Ari walked with Jackie around the Minoan ruins. "Crete," he explained, "is the birthplace of western civilization." He told her the legend of the minotaur. One of the last Minos had been married to a woman who had fallen in love with a white bull. "The result of this strange love," Ari said, "was the minotaur, who had a bull's head mounted on a human body." He added sadly, "Sometimes the sins of the parents are inherited by their blameless children."

President Kennedy was not enchanted by newspaper accounts of the fabulously luxurious cruise, with its dance bands, sixty-man crew, and two hairdressers aboard. His anger rose as Republican Congressman Oliver Bolton of Ohio, in a speech on the floor of the House, called attention to the presence aboard the yacht of Franklin D. Roosevelt, Jr. Roosevelt was then under-secretary of commerce and was thus influential with the U.S. Maritime Administration; this was surely of no little significance to Mr. Onassis and his shipping interests.

At the conclusion of the cruise, Onassis presented Jackie with a large diamond and ruby necklace. He gave the other female guests, including Lee Radziwill, pearls.

When Jackie returned to the White House she spoke ceaselessly about Onassis and his yacht. Benjamin Bradlee, a close Kennedy friend and the author of the best-selling book, *Conversations With Kennedy,* reports that Jackie said that Onassis was "an alive and vital person." Bradlee also writes that Jackie said Kennedy was being "really nice and understanding" about the cruise.

"The President did reveal that he had insisted that Onassis now not come to the United States until after 1964, the best evidence that he thinks the trip is potentially damaging to him politically," Bradlee states in his book. "But he noted that what he called 'Jackie's guilt feelings' may work to his advantage.

" 'Maybe now you'll come with us to Texas next month,' he said with a smile.

"And Jackie answered: 'Sure I will, Jack.' "

After Tina won her uncontested divorce in Alabama in 1960, Maria Callas, according to friends, appeared certain she would become the next Mrs. Onassis. Callas was spending more and more time with Onassis and less and less time on her career. Her popularity dwindled. Ari, aware of her sacrifices, conceded to a cousin, "She is my major woman."

But he still had some spare moments for other

adventures. "Ari never lost his eye or enthusiasm for women," one relative said. "Maria would usually know, but she took the situation graciously enough. She was sure of Ari's love and felt that he would always be with her."

But just as Tina had guessed wrong, so did Callas. A new threat had appeared—Jackie Kennedy.

CHAPTER VI

The Bride Wore Diamonds

Few would believe that Jackie and Ari chose one another because they fell in love. Yet from all the evidence we can find, this was indeed the case.

Extensive interviews with people who were close to the couple provide convincing evidence that each ignited the other's emotions, each satisfied the other's emotional needs, each felt happier, and more whole with the other, each felt a strong need to be with the other, and each respected the other—all of which defines love.

In London's West End, a woman who is married to a British diplomat and puts in many hours of volunteer work with children spoke about the couple. She knew Ari well, and was introduced by him to Jackie and became a close friend. "They liked each other tremendously, really and truly," she said. "Critics have insisted that the marriage was strictly a business arrangement. That's pure rot!

"Jackie does not show emotion easily or readily; yet she would lift the curtain now and then, and one could get a quick but revealing glimpse at her real feelings. Once we were lunching at the Grand Bretagne in Athens. Constantly dieting, she had ordered a salad and yogurt—and she was absolutely gushing like a young girl.

" 'He makes me come alive!' she said. 'He's so considerate. His constant attention and ingenuity are wonderful. Last Thursday morning, for instance. He told me I looked quite pale and needed a bit of a change, so he suggested we fly to Paris and have dinner at Maxim's. He's always doing things like that. He notices things others fail to see. He has such a brilliant mind and can pick up things and completely analyze them and be right.'

"Then she said it, and I shall never forget her exuberance and the way her eyes shone.

" 'It's a delightful feeling to be in love,' she told me."

Onassis was equally enthusiastic about Jackie. At Athens' very elegant and distinguished National Yacht Club, overlooking Tourcolimano Harbor, we met some other wealthy shipowners who told us how Ari would constantly drag Jackie's name into all conversations, no matter how far-fetched they were.

"We would be talking about tides," said one fleet operator whose doctor had forbidden him to drink alcoholic beverages. Nervously transferring his glass of plain tonic water from right to left hand, he said, "Ari suddenly remarked, 'Jackie's tides go from high to higher. She always operates on a very high plain— she was the real brains behind Jack Kennedy! A remarkable woman!' " The man took a sip from his glass and emitted a loud grunt that could be heard throughout the dignified club. Then he added, "It didn't sound a damn bit like Ari, but I should have known that love can make you say some damn-fool things!"

It's reported that at one luncheon, the conversation revolved around a recent best-selling book, and Ari said proudly, "Jackie wrote and published stories when she was a teenager. If she wanted to write professionally, I'm sure she'd have a great career!"

A scion of a prominent shipping family said, "We were discussing a ship's varied itinerary and that, too, set Ari off. 'Jacqueline Kennedy has the fullest itinerary you can imagine,' he said. 'How she can find time to do so much amazes me!' "

Ari contributed to that busy schedule by phoning her long distance at least once a week. From Greece, Italy, France, or wherever his business interests took him, he'd call her regularly. The conversations were lengthy and usually lasted for more than an hour— the average call cost more than two hundred dollars.

During one such phone conversation, a friend of Jackie's visiting her in her fifteen-room Fifth Avenue apartment overheard her hostess exclaim, "I speak to you so often to tell you the happenings of my day that I'm beginning to sound like Eleanor Roosevelt!" (The wife of President Franklin Roosevelt wrote a widely syndicated column called "My Day.")

When Jackie wasn't receiving phone calls from Onassis, other men were telephoning to invite her to concerts, the theater, the ballet. She had decided that the time was right for public appearances, and she accepted some of the "safe" invitations. "I wasn't ready for another marriage," she explained to a friend, "and I didn't want to get involved."

Her escorts included Robert McNamara, Averell Harriman, George Plimpton, Alan Jay Lerner, and Frank Sinatra. Jackie, who has always attracted men, once said she feels easier and safer in their presence. Some wives have said she borrows husbands as escorts as easily as some women borrow cups of sugar.

Sometimes she would be accompanied on her travels

by a male companion. With Roswell Gilpatric, the former deputy defense secretary, she explored the Yucatan Peninsula, sometimes by horseback in the moonlight. Once she was so exhilarated that she leaped into a pool with all her clothes on.

She also made an overseas trip with Lord Harlech, the former David Ormsby-Gore, a handsome widower who had been British ambassador to Washington during the Kennedy administration. Harlech had been her companion on a visit to Cambodia and the ruins of Angkor Wat in 1967.

Although he would constantly mention her name in conversations with friends, Ari kept his courtship of Jackie a secret even from his children. On several occasions when she dined with him in his penthouse apartment above Avenue Foch in Paris, he didn't even tell his servants, Helene and George, the identity of his guest. He ordered them to remain in the kitchen at all times—he served the food himself!

In late 1967, Jackie and Ari came out of hiding and made the rounds of some of New York's eating places: Mykonos, Dionysos, "21," El Morocco, and a tiny Greek restaurant in Manhattan's Greenwich Village where a jubilant Ari smashed dishes while a joyous Jackie clapped.

Although they were seen together more and more, Nevada bookmakers listed Onassis as a fifty-to-one underdog in the Jackie suitor sweepstakes.

Ari visited Jackie at her mother's summer home in Newport, Rhode Island, and announced that he, too, would like to buy a house there. He and Jackie looked at available mansions, but they couldn't find a suitable one. A real-estate agent who accompanied them said, "It was obvious that Mr. Onassis was delighted to be with her, and Mrs. Kennedy appeared to feel the same way about him. I'd guess they were in love."

In May of 1968, Jackie accepted Ari's invitation for a five-day Caribbean cruise aboard the *Christina*. At an elegant dinner party in Athens, a fellow passenger offered a rare insider's view of what it was like on the voyage. "I looked out my stateroom porthole—I was very, very lucky, for I had a magnificent view. It was early in the morning when Jackie arrived, but I could tell she knew that everyone was looking at her. She was like an actress who's performing in the center of the stage and has studied her part backward and forward. She had on a *tant soit peau* [ever so simple] brown, collarless jacket and matching skirt that was four inches above the knee—I wore mine at half an inch longer, but never Jackie! *Non!* I could tell that the suit was designed by Valentino. He, Givenchy, and Balenciaga design most of her clothes. I heard a funny story about that, in fact.

"It seems that Jackie had just returned from Paris, and reporters asked her what she had bought there.

"Jackie: 'A Givenchy and a Balenciaga.'

"Reporters: 'How very nice. May we see them?'

"Jackie: '*Certainment*. They're upstairs designing dresses.' * . . .

"She was carrying a small white box and dropped it, but a sailor quickly caught it before it hit the deck. She smiled and nodded in a most royal manner. The sailor actually bowed low as he returned the tiny box. I remembered something General de Gaulle had once said to my ex-husband—'Jacqueline Bouvier Kennedy is every inch the lady—she was born to the crown.'

"Jackie was given the Lesbos stateroom; it's the

---

* The joke, which received wide circulation that year, was originated by comedian Mort Sahl.

finest room aboard—or next to the finest. Ari has the *crème de la crème*. But the Lesbos, with its hand-painted mosaic tiles in the bathroom, priceless Louis XV antique furniture, and drapes handspun in Siam, dyed in Afghanistan, and handpainted in France, is only assigned to special guests—Sir Winston Churchill, Greta Garbo, Maria Callas, and now Jackie.

"Throughout the cruise, Ari was at her side—morning, noon, and night. Call it woman's intuition: I knew that he asked her to marry him."

When Jackie returned to the United States, she called her brother-in-law, Robert Kennedy, then in the midst of his primary campaign for the presidency. Ever since Jack's death, Bobby had been Jackie's closest adviser and confidant. She told him that she was seriously interested in Ari. The senator, who had never liked the shipping tycoon, bluntly told her that she was suffering from a schoolgirl crush and that the infatuation with "The Greek" as he called Onassis would soon pass.

One of the imponderables in the Great Mystery cannot be answered. What would Jackie have done if Bobby had lived? She trusted Bobby implicitly. After Jack died, he was a strong arm of support in her despair and anguish. When his own depression over the loss had lifted, he spent considerable time with Jackie, aiding, advising, comforting. Little wonder she once said, "I would go to hell for him."

Now, when Onassis was in Europe, he telephoned her daily. And daily he ordered huge bouquets of flowers wired to her wherever she was. Every two weeks that summer of 1968 he flew the Atlantic to be with her.

By August, he began preparing Caroline and John. Late that month, he arrived at the Kennedy compound in Hyannisport—it was his third visit that summer. It looked as it always did at that season of the year—like a children's camp in full swing.

A dozen youngsters of all ages were splashing in the swimming pool under the eyes of a lifeguard. A softball game was in progress on the broad trampled lawn. Three Kennedys were whacking a ball on the tennis court—two small ones receiving instruction from a bigger one. A half-dozen more were in the water on the private beach.

Nothing seemed to have changed, and yet life for the Kennedys had suffered another convulsive upheaval with the murder of Robert in the grimy pantry of a California hotel. Even now the tourists were coming by the hundreds, inching past the compound, descending from their cars to try to peer through the high stockade fence along Irving Avenue.

Aristotle Onassis, hands in the pockets of his white trousers, walked from the late President Kennedy's home inside the compound to meet Caroline and John, who were trotting up from the beach. The Kennedy place, once the summer White House, is on Irving Avenue, a short distance from the sprawling three-gabled residence of Rose and the late Joe Kennedy that dominates the compound. Ethel Kennedy's home is also on the grounds, but Ted and Joan have their summer place on Squaw Island, a half mile away by causeway.

On each of his visits as Jacqueline's guest, Ari had spent as much time as he could with Caroline and John—bantering with them, chatting with them on long walks, getting to know them better.

That third time, during one of their talks, Onassis told Caroline and John that their mother needed someone to look after her, someone who would be deeply and personally concerned with her problems and her welfare.

He told them that he could never replace their father, but that he would be honored to be their friend and protector, and their mother's protector too.

That was all he said then. He knew that when the time came Jackie would have to tell her children about their new father. But he was clearly preparing Caroline and John for what he hoped—what he probably strongly felt—would come very soon.

By early October, rumors were Ping-Ponging around the world. In early October, Jackie and mother-in-law Rose visited Boston's Richard Cardinal Cushing, who had married Jackie and John Kennedy fifteen years before. Great questions were involved that had to be discussed. Would Jackie suffer excommunication from the Church because Onassis was a divorced man? Word from the Vatican was that she would.

On Thursday, October 17, the Boston *Herald-Traveler* broke the news—there was to be a wedding. In Sioux Falls, South Dakota, where he had gone for the consecration of Bishop-Elect Paul Anderson, Cardinal Cushing declared, "My lips are sealed." Nevertheless, he predicted there would be an announcement soon.

There was. At 3:30 that day, Nancy Tuckerman, Jackie's social secretary, relayed a brief statement. "Mrs. Hugh D. Auchincloss has asked me to tell you that her daughter, Mrs. John F. Kennedy, is planning to marry Mr. Aristotle Onassis sometime next week."

Rose Kennedy would say nothing. Ethel declined comment. Only Ted Kennedy, through a press spokesman, issued a statement. "I talked to Jackie several days ago, and she told me of her plans. I gave her my best wishes for their happiness." Nancy Tuckerman, usually a confidante of Jackie's, was kept in the dark. She blurted to reporters, "I didn't even know until a half hour ago."

Even Mrs. Auchincloss was told virtually at the last minute. Jackie pleaded with her mother to come to Greece for the wedding, but Mrs. Auchincloss replied that it would be impossible to make arrangements that quickly.

But Jackie insisted. "I need you, Mother," she said. "Please come." Jackie wanted her mother at her side to bless the union. Finally Mrs. Auchincloss agreed to make the trip. She called off her engagements, packed, and raced to the airport.

Events moved rapidly.

A crowd of three hundred persons had gathered outside Jackie's Fifth Avenue apartment building in New York. At six P.M. on October 18, Secret Service men emerged carrying four small pieces of luggage and followed by Jackie and her two children. They entered a black limousine and drove toward the Triborough Bridge and Kennedy Airport. (Later, six trunks and suitcases were taken through a side door of the building and placed in a van.)

At 6:45, Jackie and the children reached the American Airlines terminal, which Olympic Airways used for departures. They bypassed the ticket counter and went directly to the boarding ramp, where Flight 412 was waiting. Ninety passengers had been taken off the plane to make way for the wedding party, which included Kennedy sisters Pat Lawford and Jean Smith and Mr. and Mrs. Auchincloss. (The bumped passengers left on another aircraft an hour and fifteen minutes later.) At 8:02, Jackie's plane took off for Andravida Airport, a military field about one hundred-fifty miles from Athens and an hour's flight by helicopter from Skorpios.

When Jackie emerged from her apartment building, one stout middle-aged woman called from the crowd, "I just can't believe it!" Then, like the small boy who years before had said to "Shoeless Joe" Jackson, accused of throwing games during the Black Sox baseball scandal, she added: "Say it ain't so, Jackie!"

But it was so. Jackie was on her way to marry Onassis.

It has been asserted cynically that Jackie married Ari for his wealth alone and that one need go no further in seeking an explanation. This is, in fact, probably the prevailing opinion. That Ari could provide her with an incomparable life-style goes without saying, but that this was the sole reason she chose him does total disservice to the woman. That she has expensive tastes is true; but that only a man of Onassis' means could satisfy them is absurd. Many eligible men had great wealth!

Why, then did she marry him?

Perhaps Jackie married Onassis because she found in him a man she could love.

Love, psychiatrists say, is compounded of many ingredients, not the least of which is the strength, security, and sense of permanence one finds in a marital partner.

To Jackie at that pivotal point in her life, Onassis apparently was a wall of defense against a hostile world. In 1963, with the brutal murder of her husband in an automobile seat beside her, she had discovered in one horrifying moment how fearful life can be.

In the years that followed, it seems that she found little to reassure her. "Haunted daily by an unrelenting news media," one psychiatrist says, "she probably felt injured again, this time by what she considered a hideous intrusion upon her privacy and—even more wounding to her—the privacy of her children. This is not to say that Jackie is a self-effacing woman who would choose to live her life in anonymity. She enjoys people, recognition, notoriety. Often she will court publicity while seeming to avoid it."

As one newsman once told Robert Kennedy, "Jackie wants it both ways. She insists upon her right to be left alone, but continually goes to public places, especially restaurants that she knows are patroled by gossip journalists who will see to it that she gets her name in the papers. Why doesn't she adopt the simplest solution—avoid those notoriously newsy places and eat at many restaurants where the problem of exposure is not nearly so great?"

Bobby could only offer the weak reply, "I don't see why the public cannot be courteous and give her the same right to eat where she pleases and go where she wishes as anybody else."

One can't help wondering whether Jackie truly would have wanted privacy if she could have had it after the first initial bursts of publicity. One need only point to another world-celebrated woman who sincerely desired to be left alone, and saw to it that she was—Greta Garbo.

As is often the case with celebrities, Jackie appears to have a love-hate relationship with publicity, enjoying the limelight, yet at the same time conditioned by events to feel that publicity means people around her can get hurt, even killed.

In 1968, an event occurred that apparently rekindled her terror of our hostile world and was probably responsible for her decision to marry Onassis. It was the slaying of Robert Kennedy.

After the assassination of John, Bobby took it upon himself to watch over his brother's widow. He became "passionately protective toward the woman who had glittered so brightly in the life of the brother he had idolized." * For her part, Jackie, wounded and bewildered, gratefully accepted his support.

"When Bobby was killed," a Boston psychiatrist said, "she lost someone who was very close to her. It might have been the crucial factor in her decision to marry Onassis. It would seem that she once again felt acutely alone and unprotected, that her fear of a hostile world was reignited, and that she sought a new protector. Running to a land other than her own may also have been an attempt to escape the country that, unfortunately, represented so much pain and sorrow to her."

One cannot minimize the strength Onassis offered at this critical juncture. Despite his age, he was vigorous and rugged, an earthy man of driving vitality who had proved he could face the world on its terms and come out on top. His wealth, which would enable her to hide whenever she wished from the intrusions of the world, increased the sense of security he offered.

When Jackie married Onassis, people around the world took it that she had unconsciously sought a father figure, someone like Black Jack Bouvier, someone who would fill the emotional void he had left. More analytical observers rejected the conclusion as too simplistic. But was it? "Just because something is

---

* *Ethel, the Story of Mrs. Robert F. Kennedy,* by Lester David (World 1971; Dell paperback, 1972).

simplistic doesn't mean it cannot be true," the Boston psychiatrist points out.

The question of why Onassis chose Jackie need not detain one long. That he loved her is clear from the evidence of dozens of persons who were close to them and in whom he confided. But there is another factor to be considered; for Ari, Jackie was the capstone of his career. From almost a standing start, he had accumulated nearly everything the world has to offer —fabulous wealth, the friendship of some of the most celebrated people on earth, recognition by heads of state. What better way to crown such a lifetime than by acquiring as wife the woman who had become almost a public monument—the widow of a former president, the incomparable Jackie?

Eight and a half hours after Flight 412 left Kennedy Airport on October 18, 1968, the 707 landed in western Greece. Ari ran up to the plane before the door was opened; Jackie, hatless and wearing a simple gray wool suit set off by a single strand of pearls, was one of the first passengers to emerge. Onassis kissed her on the cheek.

A Greek army sergeant who witnessed the greeting said, "I could tell that Onassis wanted to kiss her full on the lips. I hear the old man was a smart son-of-a-bitch, and when he saw her mother looking, he moved to the cheek."

Ari bowed low to the other passengers and patted Caroline on the head. He gave young John a firm handclasp and a playful blow to the jaw. Then he joined the party and told them to be ready to depart immediately. Jackie, however, said that he would have to wait while she and her children stretched their legs; then she, Caroline, and John took a walk around the airfield. When they returned, the plane took off for Preveza, where helicopters waited to take them to Skorpios.

They had deliberately avoided reporters, but a large contingent of newsmen converged on Nidri. Newsmen, warned that no uninvited person would be permitted on the island, had made plans to invade Skorpios despite the prohibition, but Onassis was prepared. He had engaged more than one hundred-fifty tough security guards and had arranged for the Greek navy to patrol the waters around the island with a large fleet of motorboats.

When a helicopter filled with newsmen hovered close to the island, two larger ones belonging to Ari intercepted it and forced it back to Nidri. Still, the journalists refused to surrender. An armada of fishing vessels filled with newspapermen, television cameramen, and magazine writers tried to storm the island. Again they were repulsed.

At this point, Jackie issued a statement to the insistent press: "We know you understand that even though people may be well-known, they still hold in their hearts the emotions of a simple person for the moments that are the most important of those we know on earth—birth, marriage, and death. We wish our wedding to be a private moment in the little chapel among the cypresses of Skorpios with only members of the family present, five of them little children. If you will give us those moments, we will gladly give you all the cooperation possible for you to take the pictures you need."

Peace was finally restored, but not until one photographer who had known Jackie in Washington and New York sent back a sour note that said, "Yes, and you undoubtedly will tell us what pictures to take!"

He explained to the other newsmen, "She never permitted us to photograph her with a cigarette in her mouth or even holding one. Although she's a heavy smoker, there are darn few pictures showing her puffing away!"

The marriage ceremony took place in the Chapel of the Little Mother of God as a light rain—which Greeks consider a sign of good luck—fell on the white-washed walls. Twenty-one guests* crowded into the tiny chapel to watch a serene Jackie exchanged vows with a slightly nervous, solemn Ari. A reporter from New York's *Women's Wear Daily,* considered to be the clothing industry's Bible, reported that Jackie's dress had been created by Valentino, the Roman couturier, and was two-piece, beige and of chiffon and lace. It had small pleats on the miniskirt. Ari wore a double-breasted, dark blue business suit and a red tie.

Caroline and John, each carrying a single slender white candle, flanked the couple. As thirty-two-year-old Archimandrite Polykarpos Athanassion of Athens' Church of Kapnikara chanted the marriage prayer, Jackie and Ari exchanged gold rings and drank red wine from a single silver chalice that symbolized their "oneness." Wreaths of white flowers were placed on the heads of the couple. Then the gold-robed prelate led them around the altar three times in the ritual dance of Isaiah.

After the couple was pronounced Mr. and Mrs. Aristotle Socrates Onassis, they left the chapel under

---

* The bride's relatives: Caroline and John; Mr. and Mrs. Hugh Auchincloss; Pat Lawford and Jean Smith; Prince and Princess Stanislas Radziwill and their two children. The bridegroom's relatives and friends: Alexander and Christina; Mrs. Artemis Garofalides, Ari's sister, who served as sponsor; Mrs. Yerasimos Patronicolous, his half-sister, and her husband; Mrs. Panos Drakos, his niece, and her husband; Mr. and Mrs. Nicholas Kokims, friends and business associates; John Georgakis, managing director of Olympic Airways, and his wife.

waiting umbrellas that shielded them from the rainfall. The new Mrs. Onassis was smiling and half-waving with one hand and holding Caroline's hand with the other. Ari said to a reporter,* "I feel very well, my boy."

The newlyweds climbed into a small yellow golf cart; Onassis drove and Caroline perched on Jackie's knees. The trio drove off to the *Christina;* John came along later.

The wedding party on Ari's yacht was in sharp contrast to the simple church ceremony. One of the guests told a Greek newspaper columnist, "Everyone was in such good spirits. I don't know when I felt so good; I clapped and sang and danced. The first dance was for Ari and Jackie—she looked so lovely. The champagne flowed and there were music and flowers and favors." There were gold bracelets for the women and gold watches for the men.

When Jackie came down for the wedding dinner, she was wearing a ring that was a huge ruby surrounded by large diamonds, and matching diamond-and-ruby earrings. She explained that they had just been given to her by Onassis. He also gave Jackie two twenty-four-karat gold bracelets, one inlaid with large rubies and diamonds. The other was a handmade replica of a Greek design from the fourth century B.C.

Caroline cried excitedly: "Mummy, Mummy, Mummy! They're so pretty. Are they real?"

They were indeed. They had cost Ari one million two hundred thousand dollars.

---

* Press coverage was limited to twelve reporters and photographers, who were kept outside the chapel by a U.S. Secret Sevice man.

CHAPTER VII

The *Christina*

Newspapers and television reports carried detailed "inside" stories about the honeymoon. The couple were swimming in Caribbean coves. They were touring the Canary Islands. They were skiing in the Swiss Alps.

Actually, Jackie and her new husband had only the briefest of honeymoons—at home on the *Christina*.

The yacht has been called one of the world's most luxurious residences on land or at sea. Not even the great palaces of the world's rulers or the homes of heads of state can match it for comforts, appointments, and the attention bestowed upon the guests invited aboard. *Money* magazine recently reported, "The paintings, antiques and other artworks are conservatively estimated to be worth twenty-five million dollars."

Sir Winston Churchill, who was once the British First Lord of the Admiralty, had sailed on many of the world's superyachts. Returning to Athens aboard the *Christina* after a cruise to the Canaries, the former prime minister said to reporters, "Ari owns the most magnificent yacht in the world—and I tell you this with firsthand knowledge."

The *Christina* carries six lifeboats, a glass-bottomed fish-watching boat, a sailboat, two kayaks, an automobile, and a seaplane. Every precaution has been taken to insure the passengers' safety. An electronic control system sounds an alarm if a porthole is opened or if the temperature in any part of the yacht rises above normal. The radio room looks like a miniature RCA communication center—after all, Ari had to keep in constant touch with his far-flung empire. By eight A.M. most mornings, he had talked to his agents in Rome, Buenos Aires, New York, and Gibraltar.

The *Christina's* sickbay is well prepared and its modern surgical and x-ray equipment is superior to that of many small hospitals. Sir Winston Churchill said of the yacht's medical facilities, "Should I suddenly develop an ailment and have to take to bed, I worry not when I'm off on a *Christina* cruise. Why, at the very least, Ari's medical apparatus is equal to that found at Guy's [a hospital in London]."

The white vessel with canary-yellow funnel and high slender bow was built in a Hamburg shipyard in 1954 and came off the ways as the Canadian naval frigate *Stormont*. With builder William Levitt's *La Belle Simone* and the *Ultima II* (owned by Charles Revson, the late cosmetics tycoon), it is one of the three largest modern private yachts in the world.* At twenty-two hundred tons, the *Christina* measures three hundred fifty-seven feet, the *Ultima II* two hundred thirty-seven and the *Simone* two hundred thirty-seven. (Levitt's yacht, though only fourteen hundred tons, is a close match for luxury. It has paneled walls, marble baths and staircases, a kidney-shaped swimming pool, an elevator with leather walls embossed in gold, a sitting room that converts into a private movie theater, and a bulkhead in the master suite that swings upward

---

* Only the yachts owned by the British and Norwegian royal families are larger. However, these vessels, built before World War II, are older.

like a garage door. Mr. and Mrs. Levitt can step onto a ladder and out onto the main deck.)

Onassis had the frigate completely refitted at Howaldtswerke in Kiel in 1954, at a cost estimated between two and a half and five million dollars. It shows. The late King Farouk of Egypt once said, "Life on the *Christina* has to be experienced to be appreciated."

Let us go, then, for a cruise—to experience, if only in the mind's eye, a glide through Grecian waters aboard this incredible ship.

The guests, most of them world celebrities, arrive singly and by twos and threes. The company could include Sir Laurence Olivier, the distinguished British actor; King Peter of Yugoslavia; Elizabeth Taylor; the Maharani of Baroda; Gregory Peck; Marlene Dietrich; Greta Garbo; Lee Radziwill; and Prince Rainier and Princess Grace. All of them have been frequent guests. (On many trips, there would also be a brace of young film actresses, obscure but moving up. Ari, usually in white trousers and dark turtleneck shirt, wearing sunglasses, would greet each personally.)

Dimi, a valet who speaks four languages, escorts the guests to their suites. There are nine, each bearing the names of Greek Islands: Andros, Crete, Lesbos, Santorini, Mykonos, Rhodes, Corfu, Chios, and Ithaca.

He is a jewel, Dimi—if he spots a hole in a garment (and, surprisingly, even celebrities have them!), he will mend it as soon as the guest leaves the cabin.

Should they need him, he says, please dial 61 on the telephone, and he will appear at once. (Once a guest reversed the numbers and dialed 16, the fire emergency extension. Seconds later, a fire brigade rushed in with hose and axes.)

Nothing escapes attention. Dimi will even ask each guest's mattress preference—soft, hard, in-between? The ship's store has dozens of custom-made ones of every type, and can change mattresses in a moment on request.

Examine in detail a typical suite—the Andros, named for the most northerly of the Cyclades chain in the Aegean:

The large bedroom is furnished with antiques gathered from all over the world. On the gold brocade walls are three small oil paintings by Old Masters, each worth tens of thousands of dollars. Against one wall is a high chest with a carved shell and fan motif. Near the fluted bed is an oval-backed gilt-wood stool; in a corner stands a small gilt settee. On the floor is a rare gold and blue carpet from Bukhara, the Uzbec province of the Soviet Union.

Adjoining the bedroom is a sitting room paneled in walnut. Furnishings include an early eighteenth-century inlaid desk and a love seat with delicately fluted legs. An early eighteenth-century Persian rug covers the floor, and pale blue satin drapes hang over the portholes.

A paneled dressing room is next to the bathroom. The latter is decorated with hand-painted blue tiles and contains a sunken tub, stall shower, bidet, flowered toilet, and a sink with knobs in the shapes of fishes.

The *Christina* can cross the ocean, but, on pleasure trips, Ari would usually order a leisurely cruise around the Greek islands at fourteen knots. The craft can step up to nineteen, but at this speed it may vibrate; Ari's command to the bridge would generally be, *"Siga*—go slowly."

By midafternoon, some of the guests are in the swimming pool on the afterdeck. It's floor, of lapis lazuli, is a reproduction of a fresco called "Minotaur and the Dancing Acrobats." At the push of a button, the floor rises nine feet, and the rich azure blue stone bottom is flush with the deck for dancing.

At five, the guests begin to gather in the bar. (From the Andros suite, go ten feet along a thickly carpeted passageway, and walk through an electrically operated door and up a teakwood stairwell.) It is a large, circular room, with stools artfully created to look like thick coils of ship's rope. The seats are covered with skin from whales' testicles, and huge whales' teeth are attached just below the bar top. The chairs have ivory arm supports carved with designs from Greek mythology. On one of the walls, enclosed in a glass case, are a large parchment world map and small models of all of Onassis' ships—each of which can be moved by pressing a lever.

On the bar is a large supply of cigarettes—there are even obscure brands should a guest desire them—another Onassis touch. There are also Cuban, Dutch, and South American cigars, and many varieties of exotic pipe tobaccos. Also on the bar are a foot-high porcelain jug in the shape of Ari's friend Winston Churchill and a slender, two-foot long series of links carved from ivory—a "sailor's whimsey."

Charlie the bartender is busy. Charlie is a fixture on the *Christina,* and his martinis are famous among the Beautiful People. He concocts them of four and one-half parts gin to seven-eighths of a part of vermouth. Those who have tasted them pronounce Charlie's martinis the world's finest.

Garbo may be on a bar stool, chatting with Ari or King Peter. Silent and uncommunicative in public, she is smiling and gracious among friends. (Incidentally, she is addressed here as Greta. On board the *Christina,* first names are used for all guests. Lord Olivier is Larry, Elizabeth Taylor is Liz.)

Dress may be formal or casual. On informal evenings, the women will wear pants—originals by Christian Dior and Yves St. Laurent are favored. Jackie once drew gasps in a *churidan*—Indian style pants, tunic, and scarf—that cost $850. Men will be casual in slacks, open shirts and sports jackets.

Time for dinner.

The all-white dining room on the main deck is about twenty-five feet square. The walls are decorated with four large oil paintings executed by French artist Marcel Vertes, some of whose works hang in the Louvre. Vertes chose Tina, Christina, and Alexander (the Onassis' children were very young at the time) to be the models for his allegorical pictures depicting the four seasons.

The dining table is round because Ari believes that round tables make for better conversation and digestion. Jackie and Ari, as hosts, sit in chairs with arms; the guests are in armless antique Louis XV seats.

At dinner parties, even among the Big Rich, one menu is generally served to all. But not at Onassis' table. He offers his guests choices. Clémont, his master chef who once ruled over the kitchen of a three-star Michelin restaurant in France usually prepares three dishes in each course.

Here is a typical menu from a dinner served in 1973:

Appetizer
   Foie Gras au Madeira
   Oysters Rockefeller à la Louisiane
   Shrimp Mogens Esbensen

Soup
 Consommé au Muscadet
 Iced Curry Soup
 Zuppa di Pesce (Italian fish soup)
Entree
 Coquilles St. Jacques
 Piece de Bouef à la Flamande
 Lamb Marrakesh
Vegetables
 Eggplant Ankara in Moussaka Skin
 Leeks in Armagnac
 Kartoffelroesti (Swiss fried potatoes)
 Baked Escarole
Dessert
 Monte Carlo Soufflé
 Avocado Ice Cream
 Poire au Chocolat
 Assorted cheeses
 Fresh fruit
 Coffee—Turkish, Brazilian, or decaffeinated
Wines
 Bourguel '59
 Chateau de Medoq '57
 Dom Perignon '64

Take an after-dinner stroll.

Leave the dining room through doors that slide open as one approaches and enter the main saloon. It is larger than the dining room and is furnished with Chippendale sofas, Queen Anne chairs, antique tables. A grand piano is in one corner. There is a Siena marble fireplace with easy chairs nearby; on the floor is an Oriental rug reportedly worth more than fifty thousand dollars. On the walls are Ari's prizes—paintings by El Greco (ranked among the great baroque masters), and Camille Pissarro and Paul Gauguin, the French impressionists. There is also a watercolor that was presented to Ari by Winston Churchill.

The walls are inlaid with lapis lazuli mosaics that took months to put in place.* Ari often told his guests a story about one of the craftsmen who installed it, who had a tendency to fall asleep on the job.

"One afternoon, he dozed off and dreamed he had died and was trying to assure the angels he belonged in heaven and not in hell. But they weren't convinced. He argued and argued, but the angels still were not sold.

"Well, as he was presenting his case, he woke up and saw me passing by. He looked and began screaming. He thought he had lost the argument and had been sent to hell—and that I was the devil!

"I think that dream must have been produced by my competitors—they are all convinced I'm the devil."

Visit the game room, which once served as a nursery for Alexander and Christina. In later years, they rarely used it, but Jackie's children did. John's electric guitar is still there; so is an ornate music box that Ari had given to Caroline. In a corner is a slot machine that came from the casino at Monte Carlo, still in perfect working order.

The main saloon is used as a movie theater. (Two years ago, Ari felt that his movie equipment needed improvement, and he had a highly-skilled technician spend several weekends aboard the *Christina* installing several advanced video-cassette receivers.) Usually a film is shown an hour after dinner; this is followed

---

* And were installed at a cost of three dollars and fifty cents a square inch, one of Onassis' biographers has estimated. At these prices, if your bedroom is fifteen feet long and has an eight-foot ceiling, it would cost you over sixty thousand dollars to duplicate the decor on just one wall.

by a midnight supper on the afterdeck adjacent to the dance floor—formerly the swimming pool. This time the chef is a Greek who has worked in some of the finest restaurants in Athens. The buffet style supper is another culinary masterpiece. There is *Keftethis* (Greek meat balls), *Taramasalata* (fish roe), *Avogolemono* (fish broth), *Aginares* (artichokes), and *Dolmades* (grape leaves stuffed with meat and rice). There are also *Peínerli* (tiny pizzas filled with cheese, chopped meat, or sausage), *Visina* (black cherries), *Fráoula* (strawberry-flavored grapes), *Próveio yaórti* (yogurt with honey), and *Baklava* and *Galaktoboureko* (pastry with honey and nuts).

Champagne? Of course—and served with a delicate nut bread. The evening may end quietly, usually between one and two A.M., but on special occasions there may be raucous, joyous Greek dancing. Once, while aboard ship, Ari received word that he had been awarded the Dag Hammarskjold Gold Medal for Industrial Merit. "This calls for a celebration!" he announced to his guests.

He walked to the center of the dance floor and, as *bouzouki* musicians played a *chassapiko*—a Greek dance—he raised his hands over his head and snapped his fingers rapidly. His feet turned at forty-five-degree angles; he moved them gracefully from left to right and back again. The tempo of the music increased. Ari waved his arms to the men, inviting them to join him. Soon all the men in the room were dancing. Ari glided to the buffet table, grabbed plates, and dashed them to the floor. The others followed suit. The musicians strummed faster and faster. When the dance ended, Ari walked off the china-littered floor to the applause of his company.

By two A.M., most of the guests have said good night and are in their suites.

Jackie has climbed the delicately curving stairs to her private quarters on the bridge deck. She has a three-room apartment furnished with rare antiques—there is an amethyst Buddha, one of only two in the world, worth an estimated three hundred thousand dollars; several Russian icons; and an El Greco valued at eight hundred thousand dollars. The semicircular bathroom alone is worth noting. The fixtures are of solid silver and gold, and the marble bath is a duplicate of one found in the palace of an ancient Minoan king on the island of Crete. The walls are inlaid with mosaics of dolphins and flying fish.

Four hours later, Ari, bare to the waist, is in his office aboard ship, working at his eighteenth-century black lacquered desk. The guests sleep as the *Christina* glides across the glassy Aegean.

CHAPTER VIII

Man and Wife

Not even the driving rain could dim the grandeur of the wedding reception aboard the *Christina*. Ari, sipping Scotch, walked happily through the throng of guests, greeting them, urging caviar and champagne upon them. Thirteen girls from nearby Lefkas danced; *bouzouki* music flowed throughout the great, gaily-lit vessel.

The rain pelted down and the wind rose as the party went on. Toward dawn, with the ship rocking in a heavy sea, the wedding party at last bade farewell to their guests. Jackie had changed into slacks and a beige pullover; Ari wore slacks and an open-necked shirt.

They hugged Caroline and John, kissed Alexander and Christina, and shook hands with all the friends and relatives, who then crossed the span of heavy water by speedboat to Nidri, went by car to Aktion Airport, and from there went to Athens.

Then the newlyweds retired.

The Kennedy contingent checked into the Grand Bretagne, where Caroline and John were put to bed while the other members of the wedding party threw a vodka bash on the hotel's second floor. When newsmen swept through the corridors seeking them out, young John opened the door of his bedroom and called out, "Don't let the press in!" Secret Service agent John Walsh quickly pulled him back inside.

Some Greeks, with their powerful family instincts, were sharply critical of the Onassises for "dumping" the two small children in a hotel with only a governess to care for them. An Athens woman was quoted in a newspaper as saying, "I can understand that the newly-weds want to be alone. And I can understand when a couple without money have to leave their children in someone else's care. But considering the size of the Onassis yacht, it seems incredible that the children should receive such treatment."

The captain of the *Christina* was prepared to set out on a honeymoon cruise on three hours' notice, but no orders came.

The bridegroom was too busy to go away. He had interrupted a major deal with the Greek government to be married. The day after the ceremony, he left the *Christina* in the morning, boarded his private Piaggio plane, and flew to Athens for meetings with Prime Minister George Papadopoulos. He returned in late afternoon but left again the following day.

The final meeting was held in the prime minister's limousine while they rode through the streets of Athens. In the car, the two men shook hands on a four-hundred-million-dollar deal under which Onassis agreed to construct a huge oil refinery and an aluminum plant in Greece in return for special government concessions.

What was the marriage like?

A picture has been pieced together from accounts of incidents that occurred on Skorpios, on board the *Christina,* at the villa in Glyfada (a fashionable Athens suburb), at Jackie's Fifth Avenue apartment, at Ari's London townhouse, at his Monte Carlo office, and in other places where the couple went to rest and play. Glimpses of Jackie and Ari as man and wife were obtained from dozens of persons close to the couple— servants, ex-servants, relatives, waiters, doormen, friends and former friends, present and former employees, and others who served, watched, and did business with the famous couple.

It is astonishing to discover that Ari, the cosmopolite who had been everywhere, had seen much, and knew life and people, was actually tormented by jealousy.

Several of Jackie's friends disclosed that he wanted to know about her previous attachments. Particularly, he would ask probing questions about Lord Harlech. Had there been a romantic involvement? Had they really been only friends? The subject seemed to cause him great anguish. Again and again, he would find excuses to bring up the subject.

One woman said, "I thought Ari was a man of the world, but at times he'd act like a jealous, heartsick kid and try to pump me about Lord Harlech or some other men he thought Jackie had once favored."

She added, "Another concern was Jackie's first husband. Ari would pretend to be asking political questions, but it was as if he hoped to trap Jackie into saying that she had preferred J.F.K. to him."

Politics could not be a major topic of conversation because, while Ari was deeply interested in political cross-currents and their meanings, Jackie made it abundantly clear that she was not. However, on occasion Onassis would launch into a discussion of the American presidency and its problems.

He gave former President Dwight D. Eisenhower low marks because, he said, "Ike didn't know the meaning of loyalty." He felt that Ike had not supported his chief of staff, Sherman Adams, in 1958 when the textile millionaire Bernard Goldfine admitted that he had presented Adams with gifts, including a vicuna coat. Adams, for nearly six years the most powerful man in government, left office quietly a few months after the case exploded. "He should have stood by Sherman Adams," Ari insisted, "just the way I would if one of my trusted employees got into hot water."

Ari did discuss the Watergate scandal with his wife. Along with many Americans, Ari thought Nixon was "plain stupid not to burn those tapes." He added, "He could have burned them and then said he did it to prevent innocent people from getting hurt, and that the presidency has to be inviolate." Then he added cynically, "Crap like that. I'll bet he'd have gotten away with it. But the man was plain stupid."

Jackie could be impulsively affectionate. Once, while both were reading on the deck of the *Christina,* Jackie suddenly rose from her reclining chair, walked over to her husband, and kissed him.

Surprised, he asked, "What's that for?"

She explained that she was overwhelmed because he had stayed up the previous night when her son, John, had a stomachache. "I just thought about it," she said. She walked over to Ari again and kissed him several more times. Then she sat down and resumed reading.

A moment later, he walked over to her. He reached down and gave her a thumping kiss.

"I just remembered," he said, "that a couple of months ago I was ill and you stayed up with me." They both laughed and kissed again.

Another time, soon after the death of Alexander, Onassis was looking at a picture of his son taken when the boy was about six years old. The child was

Onassis with his family in 1957

Jackie and J.F.K. in New York, 1961

Onassis and Maria Callas

Jackie, Ari, and Caroline after the wedding

*Alexander and Christina at Jackie and Ari's wedding
reception on the* Christina

Mr. and Mrs. Aristotle Onassis

*John, Jackie, Caroline, Rose, Ted, and
Janet Auchincloss*

Tina Onassis and son Alexander

Jackie in the garden of Ari's house in Athens

At the Neraida Club, Athens

The last photo of father and son, 1973

*Stavros Niarchos and Tina at Alexander Onassis'
funeral*

Onassis shortly before his death

Christina and Jackie at Ari's funeral

Jackie and son John at Ari's funeral

Christina and her husband, Alexander S. Andreadis

seated behind the wheel of a toy car. Tears welled in Ari's eyes as he stared at the photo. Jackie, sitting nearby, rose, threw her arms around him, and kissed him. He held her closely.

During their six years of marriage, Jackie and Ari had many disagreements about matters not unfamiliar to other husbands and wives—money, children, and personal habits.

How many fathers around the world, for example, have objected to blue jeans? Ari did too. Once, when he and Jackie were in the *Christina's* bar, he complained about the jeans that Caroline and John wore as often as most other teenagers. "I suppose if I have to learn to put up with those ridiculous-looking jeans, I have to," he said resignedly. "But tell me, why in the world do they always have to be so dirty?"

Jackie made no response. Next morning, she appeared at breakfast in a pair of faded jeans. She smiled at Ari and pirouetted several times. He looked at her, then smiled resignedly. "Well," he said, "at least they're clean."

To Jackie, even wearing jeans was an elaborate production. She had to choose the proper casual blouse, hairdo, perfume—and, of course, sneakers with the appropriate number of holes. Maude Shaw, Caroline's governess in the White House, says Jackie has always taken great pains with her appearance. "She would no more see her husband until she fixed her hair and her face," recalls Miss Shaw, "than Queen Elizabeth would receive the prime minister wearing a bathrobe."

Friends of Jackie agree. "At all times, Jackie would dress ever so carefully," said a former neighbor. "Be it blue jeans or a Balenciaga creation, it had to be A-1 perfect. I remember when we were both living on

N Street [in Washington, D.C.] and the children were playing in the sandbox. It would be Jackie's turn to supervise them, and she'd come out looking radiant. I used to think I was such a schlump compared to Jackie."

At first, like all new husbands, Ari was tolerant. But after the first few months, he became increasingly irritated when he was forced to wait endlessly while Jackie primped.

Once Jackie swept into the Athens Hilton Hotel wearing her hair in ultrafashionable bouffant style and in very high-heeled shoes. That evening, she evidently had taken special pains with her appearance and her normal height of five feet six inches was increased almost to six feet.

Ari followed closely behind. Guests in the lobby tittered at their Mutt-and-Jeff appearance. Ari heard and hurried on, not bothering to hold the door open for his wife. Later that evening, a waiter overheard their conversation. "He was very mad," the waiter said. "He tell her not to do it again. I see she take shoes off, but when they go out, she put shoes on. Ari mad again!"

Jackie worried constantly about her children's safety; kidnapping was her overriding concern. When Caroline reached her sixteenth birthday, she lost her Secret Service protection. Private guards were engaged, but Jackie felt Ari was not doing enough to insure Caroline's safety. She also felt he wasn't spending enough time with the children.

Once at an Athens nightclub, a waiter reveals, Jackie told Ari, "You're away so often, they don't even know you exist!"

Ari replied that he had gone out of his way to be a good stepfather. "I've given them everything they ever wanted," he protested. "Ponies, boats, cameras! Why, I've even flown their friends thousands of miles so that they could be with them! I've given those kids more attention than I gave my own children."

Early in January 1972, London newspapers reported that Jackie had had a shouting battle with Ari in London's Heathrow Airport. It began when they entered a Pan-Am VIP lounge, the Clipper Club. There were no other passengers present, and when the argument became heated, Ari ordered the staff into an adjoining kitchen and shut the door.

One Pan-Am employee said, "It sure was a flaming row. She was shouting at him to be quiet and to listen for once. It wasn't at all one-sided, take it from me. It got so loud that I don't think they could even hear each other."

Finally, Jackie ran out of the lounge and got into a car. She sat there and angrily thumbed through a magazine until a Pan-Am official told her that it was time to board the plane. As Jackie walked toward the airliner, according to one news account, she was heard to announce loudly, "I'm going home to America!"

The seat next to her had been purchased for a Mr. Simpson—Onassis often traveled under that assumed name (Perhaps a Freudian analyst can explain why they chose the name of a woman—Wallis Warfield Simpson—whose marriage was the only one in this century to cause a worldwide sensation equal to the one *their* marriage caused.) This time, however, no one used the seat. A spokesman for Ari denied that Onassis was Mr. Simpson or that he had ever intended to fly to America, and said that the small suitcase he had carried to the airport was just full of important papers he intended to use in London.

During her marriage to Ari, Jackie amassed a large,

extremely valuable jewelry collection, but she would sometimes misplace pieces, and once she allowed Caroline to play catch with one of her diamond rings. The youngster dropped it, and the ring rolled away. The servants looked for the ring, but it was not to be found. When Ari was told about the missing ring he was upset, and he, too, looked for it. Again no luck. (Later, a servant found the ring under a carpet.)

Many of the couple's quarrels revolved around Jackie's spending habits. Apparently she had a lifelong pattern of overspending. When she was earning sixty dollars a week as reporter-photographer for the now-defunct Washington *Times-Herald,* she spent about twice that sum on clothes. Pulitzer Prize-winning journalist Fred Sparks reported in *The $20,000,000 Honeymoon* that John Kennedy once asked a friend, "Isn't there a Shopper's Anonymous?"

When she was First Lady, writes Mary Barelli Gallagher,* her personal secretary at the time, Jackie spent one hundred twenty-five thousand dollars a year, the bulk of it on clothes. In 1961, her personal expenses between April and June amounted to thirty-five thousand dollars, half for clothes alone. "Clothing was her blind spot," wrote Mrs. Gallagher. "So were paintings and house furnishings, especially antiques. If Jackie liked something, she ordered it and coped with the bills later." The president, as might be expected "blew up." Jackie promised to reform, but the spending continued unabated.

Although Ari gave Jackie a thirty-thousand-dollar-a-month allowance and permitted her charge accounts, she was always running short. She raised extra cash by selling little-used possessions to secondhand stores.

---

* *My Life With Jacqueline Kennedy,* by Mary Barelli Gallagher.

The chief buyer of a Manhattan store that does a brisk selling business for the former First Lady says, "Jackie has been dealing with us for a long time. It started when Jack was a senator, continued when he became president, and went on during the Onassis marriage. She still does business with us.

"The way it works is like this—she'll telephone and we'll go to her apartment on Fifth Avenue to look over the items she wants us to sell. We'll agree on how much they should sell for, and then we'll send over a truck to pick up the clothes. When they are sold, Jackie gets half of the proceeds.

"She always has loads of very good things. Some have never been worn, or only worn two or three times. I remember an original Valentino gown she had worn once at a very important function. Some very lucky person got that gown for two hundred fifty dollars—it cost at least ten times that sum!"

Shortly before Ari's death, Jackie raised money by auctioning off a number of family belongings, among them a chair with the circular emblem of the Choate School on the back. (President Kennedy attended the fashionable prep school from 1931 to 1935.) The William Doyle Galleries of East 87th Street in New York auctioned it for three hundred dollars. Old nursery furniture once used by son John was also sold at auction.

In 1971, an Italian magazine called *Playmen* published fourteen nude photos of Jackie. On nine pages of the magazine were color pictures showing the former First Lady sunning herself and walking around Skorpios without any clothes on. The magazine's editor said it was the work of ten photographers equipped with underwater cameras and telescopic lenses.

It was rumored that Ari had offered to buy the

negatives for a quarter of a million dollars, although Ari told reporters, "I have to take my pants off to put on my bathing suit. Well, so does Jackie!"

To friends, he said proudly, "She looks so lovely without clothes. Just look at that figure; I think I'll get an artist to paint her. She makes all the other nude ladies look like bags of bones."

Jackie told a reporter for *Newsweek* magazine, "I don't treat it as a reality. It doesn't touch my real life, which is with my children and my husband. That's the world that's real to me."

Discussing the matter on the telephone with a friend, she was heard to remark, "Did you know that Kirk Douglas paid one hundred dollars for a copy of the magazine?" A pause. Then Jackie said to her caller, "Thank you for thinking I'm worth a lot more. You keep on thinking it."

At a New York cocktail party, John Kenneth Galbraith, the former ambassador to India and a close friend of Jackie's, teased her. "I didn't recognize you with your clothes on."

CHAPTER IX

Skorpios

A year after the Skorpios wedding, Onassis told reporters, "Jackie is like a little bird that needs its freedom as well as security. She gets both from me. We trust each other implicitly."

The statement started divorce rumors flying. Headlines in an English newspaper announced: JACKIE AND ARI READY TO SPLIT. HE ADMITS JACKIE NEEDS FREEDOM!" Other articles forecasting a breakup began appearing.

The couple continued to live their normal jet-set lives: Jackie in New York and Ari in Greece; Jackie in France and Ari in Egypt; Jackie in Greece and Ari in New York. But they would always meet after a short time and spend time together on the island of Skorpios.

During these periods, the couple still appeared to be very much in love. There are many photographs of them dining in restaurants that seem to prove this tender devotion; people who aren't in love do not kiss impetuously at breakfast over the criossants and coffee. Nor do they bring gifts of the most expensive gems.

"He continued to literally bombard Jackie with jewelry," says the woman friend who had been present on the Caribbean cruise prior to their marriage. "He had a standing order at one Athens store to deliver her flowers with a bracelet or necklace whenever he was away."

Occasional quarrels erupted, but there were many moments of tenderness. Jackie and Ari were seen dining together frequently, chatting intimately, smiling at one another. Once in a restaurant in the south of France, they noticed a young American couple struggling over a French menu. Ari whispered to Jackie, walked over to the table, bowed, and asked if he could help. He then offered his recommendations. The couple, who appeared to be newlyweds, were astonished when they realized who their interpreter was. They stammered their thanks and took Ari's advice. Ari bowed again and returned to Jackie. He then had the waiter send over a bottle of rare vintage wine to the young couple's table. Jackie beamed at him.

Still, the rumors continued. Ari told one reporter, "Whenever I take a suitcase or sneeze, the papers say that I'm getting a divorce or that I'm about to die! It's all a pack of bullshit!"

Jackie was more ladylike in dealing with the press. She wouldn't offer much information, but she did dole it out in a most dignified fashion. Once an English newsman asked her, "It is true that you and Mr. Onassis are apart so much because you find it a strain to be together?"

Jackie replied, "We are very busy people, and at times our work takes us to opposite shores. I'm sure you don't see your wife constantly!"

A French journalist asked Jackie some other direct questions. "Are you sorry now that you entered into this strange marriage, and do you intend to end it?"

Jackie: "The answer to both your questions is a big fat no. Mr. Onassis and I are still very much in love. And furthermore, we don't regard the marriage as strange. Good day."

On one of the few occasions when she gave a more involved reply she was in Tehran, where she and her multimillionaire husband were taking a business holiday. Ari was hoping to get special oil concessions, and Jackie wanted to do some exploring. The former First Lady appeared to be in gay spirits and was delighted to answer questions. When asked if there was a difference between being Mrs. John Kennedy and being Mrs. Aristotle Onassis, she replied, "People often forget that I was Jacqueline Lee Bouvier before being Mrs. Kennedy or Mrs. Onassis. Throughout my life, however, I've always tried to remain true to myself. And I'll continue to do this as long as I live. I am today what I was yesterday and with luck what I will be tomorrow."

On their fourth anniversary, Jackie gave Ari a "surprise party" at New York's El Morocco. The "surprise" soon leaked to him when Jackie began inviting dozens of guests, who included: Rose Kennedy, Mr. and Mrs. Stephen Smith, Lee Radziwill, Oleg Cassini, William Buckley, Doris Day, director Mike Nichols, cartoonist Charles Addams, Reza Fallah (chief of Iran's oil interest), George Moore (former chairman of the First National City Bank and president of the Metropolitan Opera)—and about fifty other notables.

It was a sumptuous affair.

They began with cocktails and imported mushrooms stuffed with snails, bacon-wrapped chicken livers, and heart-shaped Swedish meatballs. After the hors d'oeuvres, the guests were ushered into the Champagne Room, where pink-covered tables seating eight people glowed under soft pink lights that were reflected from crystal sconces and flickering candles. Jackie and Ari sat at separate tables.

The dinner: Russian caviar served with blini and vodka; and consommé vermicelli; controfilet with truffle sauce, endives, and beet salad; and cherries jubilee. The wine was Chateau Simard St. Emilion 1967 and Pol Roger 1964 champagne.

At one A.M., the party started breaking up, and the Onassises went down to the main section of the restaurant, where they sat at their usual corner table. They drank some more champagne—Rene Lalou 1966. At 2:30 Ari got their wraps and they went out to get into their waiting Rolls-Royce. Spectators who were lined up outside El Morocco applauded and sang, "Happy anniversary to you . . . happy anniversary, dear Ari and Jackie—happy anniversary to you!"

Ari applauded the crowd, European style. Jackie tossed kisses.

Late one afternoon, Onassis was strolling along a path on Skorpios with a fellow Greek shipping magnate. Stopping at the water's edge, he pointed to Sparti Island, a blob of land about a mile from where they stood.

"It's mine," Ari said. "I bought it to keep strangers from watching me pee."

Owning an island is a clear sign in Greek shipping circles that one has arrived. But possessing a *second* island to insure the privacy of the first is the kind of oneupmanship only Aristotle Onassis could practice on his colleagues. When he acquired Skorpios he also bought nearby Sparti, but he had no intention of developing the place. He merely wanted to make sure he wouldn't be troubled by neighbors.

During his life, Onassis owned many homes and

estates in all parts of the world, among them an exquisite villa in the fashionable Athens seaside resort of Glyfada; a townhouse in London; a hacienda in Montevideo, Uruguay, a penthouse on the Avenue Foch in Paris; a lodge in Buenos Aires; an apartment in the Hotel Pierre in New York; and a mansion in Monte Carlo.

But of them all, Skorpios was his crown jewel. Ari would have preferred Ithaca, the forty-one-square-mile island in the Ionian Sea believed to have been the birthplace and later the kingdom of Ulysses, the hero of Homer's *Odyssey*. But Ithaca, unfortunately, was inhabited—sparsely, to be sure, by fewer than two thousand persons, but peopled nonetheless, and Ari wanted total privacy. Besides, Ithaca was not for sale.

So he sent emissaries to scout the waters of the Aegean and the Ionian. It was a real-estate hunt of formidable scope, considering that there are over fourteen hundred islands in the Aegean, the vast majority unsettled and undeveloped. His men explored the northern Sporades, the Dodocanese, the Cyclades, and the Saronics, and they island-shopped westward through the Sea of Crete and up into the Ionian. But they saw nothing suitable until one day they came upon a scorpion-shaped, five-hundred-acre isle ten miles north of Ithaca.

With its lush greenery, the island looked tropical, but it was hardly a paradise. The parts that weren't rocky were thickly overgrown; there were no roads, not even a pathway through the vegetation. The tall pines and cypresses blotted out the sun, giving the place such a look of intense gloom that all the scouts could think of as they surveyed the acreage was, "What a good place to have a funeral!" Worse, the island had no water supply of its own.

Nonetheless, it was available, and since it was the best of what they had been able to discover, one scout told Ari about it, if with little enthusiasm.

"But he came down and liked it at once," the scout said. "His eyes saw what mine had not—he could look at this overgrown piece of land and visualize what could be done with it."

In 1962, Ari paid sixty thousand dollars for the island, and at once the reconstruction began. Road-builders and landscape architects roamed over the scorpion-shaped island. Soon came the bulldozers, cranes, steam shovels, and other earth-movers, manned by hundreds of workers. After several years, at a cost of three million dollars, the rocky pile had been transformed into a private pleasure dome. The water supply? No problem. Reservoirs were constructed on the highest point; they would be replenished daily with water hauled in by boat.

Skorpios is dominated by The House,* a magnificent dwelling that was designed for Onassis by a prize-winning architect whom Ari instructed to make the villa as impregnable as possible to all natural violence —nearby islands had been devastated ten years earlier by a severe earthquake. Ari insisted that the foundation be "almost as thick as that of the Empire State Building!"

The house is a low, two-story, rambling cement building surrounded by hundreds of rose bushes, bougainvilleas, and jasmine. It has fourteen rooms, including a modern stainless-steel kitchen, five spacious

---

* Onassis used to speak of it as Persian-style and told the architect that he wanted it to resemble a palace he had once seen in Iran (formerly Persia). Ari described it carefully and was pleased with the results. Just as the mansion was completed, he started speaking of constructing a much bigger and more elaborate structure, but it never materialized.

bedrooms, each with dressing rooms, and a large living-dining room combination. Ari spent many hours in an armchair in the living room, puffing on a silver-covered waterpipe and looking at the gardens—he had insisted that something be in bloom throughout the year. One of the servants told us that Ari's favorite chair was shifted about ten feet when Jackie ordered Christina's grand piano moved into its spot. Ari sulked for days.

He and Jackie had different floral preferences and would often argue about the kinds and colors of the blooms in the gardens. After Ari's death, she reportedly ordered the flowers changed.

There is a large patio in the rear of the house with many bucket-type wicker chairs. The chairs were reportedly made to accommodate all posterior sizes—thin, medium, fat, and very fat. ("Ari try to do something for everybody," a crew member said.)

Not far from the main house are ten ultramodern guest chalets, each containing three bedrooms, a sitting room, bath and individual gardens. "Ari always had a great interest in flowers," his cousin said. "Like many Greek people, he believed that blooming roses indicated glad tidings. He used to say that before a big deal he would go to Rhodes, because it was named after roses and that it was a lucky omen."

To the right of the guest compound, on a bluff near the smaller harbor, is the seventy-five-year-old Chapel of Panagitsa, deteriorating when Ari purchased the island. Ari had it restored to its former simple elegance. Nestled between several massive cypress trees, it is white-washed except for a dark-stained door surmounted with a classic pediment, or low triangular gable that ancient Greeks used to crown the entranceway of their temples. The pediment is repeated in the roofline.

Mrs. Kyria Maria, wife of the chief gardener, looks after the small church and keeps it immaculate. She said, "Mr. Onassis wanted everything very clean. So even if the chapel is almost never used, it is always very clean and ready!" The body of Aristotle Onassis lies to the left of the chapel under a cypress tree. His son, Alexander, is buried to the right of the chapel.

There is a servant's house near the chapel, but most of the employees are ferried daily from Nidri. They arrive at dawn and leave at dusk. Further along are two greenhouses and the Onassis farm with Shetland ponies, Arabian stallions, sheep, goats, chickens, pigs, turkeys, and geese. Ari also built an airfield; it is small but aviation authorities approve of it because it meets the strictest safety specifications. There are also several large garages for the island's twenty automobiles.

On the southwest tip of Skorpios is the "family" beach and a modest white stucco house called "La Taverna." Four steps lead to the first floor, each with beautiful potted plants on the sides. Several years ago, a guest tripped on a plant and complained. Ari's solution—not to remove the flowerpot, but never to invite the guest again.

Onassis crisscrossed the island with six miles of macadamized roads and numerous foot paths and riding trails, often hewing through solid rock. The northern part has been left mostly in its natural state except for the roads. During the early years of their marriage, Jackie and Ari would come here often, on horseback or strolling hand in hand on paths lined by laurel, myrtle, and oleander.

Onassis cultivated the many hundreds of olive trees originally on the island and brought in hundreds more. Proudly he would tell his guests that they produce thirty thousand pounds of olive oil each year. He also added to the island's grape vines from which a bitter-sweet wine is made. No visitor to Skorpios ever left without tasting the oil and the wine at the urging of Onassis.

At midpoint in their marriage, Ari seemed to be trying extraordinarily hard to please his wife. When she enthused over the singing of a currently popular Greek star, Stamatis Kokotas, he brought the entertainer to Skorpios for a private performance. At other times, he imported dancers and musicians to the island for Jackie's pleasure. Once she expressed interest in meeting some of the astronauts—immediately he extended an invitation to them, but it was vetoed by President Nixon.

When Onassis' business took him away for several days, Jackie would fly to Athens, where she would spend hours at the National Archeological Museum on Tositza Street. The museum contains one of the most famous of all archeological finds, the gold death mask of Agamemnon. Jackie's favorite displays were an exhibition of royal tombs excavated in the 1800s and a bas-relief of Demeter, the Greek earth-goddess of corn, harvest, and fruitfulness, handing an ear of corn to Triptolemus, and agricultural hero and the legendary inventor of the plough.

At home, Mr. and Mrs. Onassis would play two-handed card games, hold hands while viewing movies flown over from the United States, England, and France, and spend many hours talking about their children. Sometimes they would take a small launch and dine at Nikos' taverna.

Ari preferred local food—*meze*—cheese, olives, and cucumber; *synagrida*—slices of grilled sea bass; *souzoukakia*—balls of meat and rice in a sauce;

Guivetsi—roast lamb with pasta; and *vlita*—broiled dandelions served with olive oil and lemon. Jackie, a devotee of French *haute cuisine,* was not fond of Greek cooking. One day, however, she decided to sample some at Nikos'—and liked it. Ari reacted with glee. "He so happy he break plates," Nikos reports.

Late in July 1970, Ari was on Skorpios when he received an urgent phone call: Olympic Airways Flight 255, en route from Beirut to Athens, had been seized by six Arab terrorists. The Boeing 727, with forty-nine passengers and a crew of six, had been forced to land at the Athens airport. The hijackers, armed with five pistols, two hand grenades, and a submachine gun, were demanding the immediate release of seven Arab terrorists being held prisoner in Greece. Unless the Greek government complied at once, they threatened to blow up the plane with all aboard.

Ari immediately flew to Athens in his private five-seater amphibian plane, and, with Stylianos Pattakos, the Greek deputy premier and interior minister, attempted to negotiate with the hijackers. He offered himself as a hostage in exchange for the prisoners, but his offer was rejected.* The air pirates' reply, reported in *Newsweek,* was, "Who is Onassis? Never heard of him!"

Told who he was, the hijackers still spurned his offer. "They said I was only one," Ari reported afterward, "while the passengers were many. It seems that my stock is falling."

Later, Jackie teased him with: " 'Who is Onassis? Never heard of him!' "

---

* After eight tense hours of negotiations with the Greek government, the hijackers accepted a guarantee that the terrorists would be freed within one month. Onassis walked out to the plane and handed over a signed note. "I talked," he said later, "while a guy held a tommygun pointed at me."

What was Jackie's daily routine on Skorpios? Servants and guests reported her schedule.

If she rose late in London, New York, Paris, and other places, angering Ari, on the island things were different—she would rise at nine. For breakfast, she would have tea, orange juice, and toast brought to bed. Then:

9:45	Exercise (including standing on head)
10:00	Swim and sunbathing
11:30	Freshen up for lunch
12 noon	Light lunch—salad, hamburger or small steak, tea or skimmed milk
1:00 P.M.	More sunbathing and relaxing time
3:00	If Ari or children in residence, riding sailing, walking
5:00	Swim
6:00	Cold nonalcoholic drink—iced tea without sugar or diet cola
6:30	Relaxation and dress for dinner (more time required if Ari or friends on island)
8:00	Drinks—Jackie: daiquiri; Ari: martini
9:00	Dinner
10:30	Card-playing, reading, or viewing a movie
11:30	Retire for night.

Revealing insights into Jackie's changing moods and interests were described by a close friend, wife of a retired corporate executive, who has known her for many years.

"The first time I visited Skorpios," she said, "Jackie raved about Greece. She didn't seem to be interested in news about home. She spoke only about the beauties of Greece. Caroline and John were there at the time, and Jackie wasn't tense in handling them. I remember how I'd admired her way with them—I had never had that relationship with my children (I have three). Caroline would ask for something and Jackie's reply was easy—she was more like a friend than a mother.

"Jackie insisted on showing me the sights, and we took one of the boats to the mainland. A chauffeur-driven car is always waiting! We drove along with Jackie holding forth on a variety of things. Once she said, 'I know our country has a lot to offer, but do you honestly think it compares to this?' She held her hands aloft and continued, 'This is God's country!' When we got outside, she picked a wildflower and handed it to me. 'Here's a part of it!' she said. At that time, the marriage appeared as sunny as the skies above the Ionian Sea in June."

CHAPTER X

Caroline, John, and Other Kennedys

After "Why did they marry each other?" the question most often asked about the Ari-Jackie union was, "How did Caroline and John feel about their new stepfather?"

Caroline, remembering John Kennedy, was reportedly antagonistic. But as the years went on, each grew increasingly fond of the rough-hewn multimillionaire, and it became a fondness approaching love.

Onassis, as we have seen, tried to prepare the children for a new father. He knew that he could never assume the role of a real parent, but he determined from the start to be unfailingly kind to them and, more important, to attempt to understand them. All of us do better with second, third, and later children than we do with the first, having learned by our mistakes. Onassis was no exception. He bungled in rearing Alexander and Christina, overwhelming them with luxuries instead of what they most needed and wanted —his time and attention. With his new family, he determined to avoid the error. Lemoyne K. Billings, a classmate of President Kennedy's at Choate and a close family friend, said: "Onassis made a big effort to be a good father."

He made a bigger effort than the press gave him

credit for; note, for example, the story of the gift horse. Ari, busy winding up a major deal, heard that Caroline had her heart set on acquiring one. Reportedly he told Jackie, "Buy her the horse. Don't worry about expense—I'll pay the bill. Buy the horse's mother and sisters and brothers." The story, which received wide circulation, was intended as dramatic illustration that Ari believed in checkbook child-rearing.

The truth is that Jackie purchased the horse, but Onassis cut short his business so that he could fly to the United States and be present when Caroline received her gift. He knew the gift would mean much more to her this way than if it were presented in absentia.

Yet, try as he would, he found that his life and those of the children were—literally—worlds apart. John was attending school in New York, Caroline in Massachusetts, and Onassis traveled all over the globe running his vast shipping empire and other business interests. Therefore, the circumstances prevented the development of a close father-child relationship. It is probable that Caroline and John found the father-image they needed not in their Greek stepfather but in other males around them, chiefly their Uncle Ted and the friends of their late father, who made it a point to see them as often as possible.

Both youngsters spent many of their vacations on Skorpios and saw Onassis on his many visits to New York. Ari bought them many gifts, taking the trouble to find out in advance from the Kennedys if there was "something special" they would like.

When Caroline's friends were visiting, he would chat with them, ask questions about their school and activities, make jokes. Her friends told us that he was unfailingly warm and cordial. "He was such a *nice* man," said one pretty brunette classmate. "I liked him a lot."

In the end, Onassis succeeded in the difficult task of being a stepfather. After he died, Caroline confided to Juan Cameron, a boyfriend during her senior year at Massachusetts Concord Academy, "I didn't see him that much, but I really did love him." One can speculate about the depth of love, or what the word actually means to a seventeen-year-old, but there cannot be any doubt that there was affection and that it ran deep.

As for John, he and Ari were *filaracos*—buddies. This is a word the boy himself used to describe their closeness. On Skorpios, the two would often go fishing, sailing, or waterskiing together and thoroughly enjoy the time spent in each other's company.

Ari used to delight John with stories about pirates and sunken treasure. One was the spinetingling tale of thirty ships sunk in Hawaiian waters. Recently, John and his cousin Timothy Shriver spent three days in Hawaii, where John said, "We dived as deep as one hundred eighty feet and saw lots of the thirty sunken ships."

Nikos Kominates said, "I think maybe John make up a little for Ari's dead son, Alexandros. John, Ari together lot. I teach John speak Greek. I hear John say to Ari, '*Thela na fao* on the *Christina*—I want to eat on the *Christina*.' Ari laugh loud because John speak part Greek, part American. Sometimes, I take Caroline, John fishing; they no catch fish. John ask me show Ari my fish catch and say that his. I do. Ari say, 'John, you good fisherman!' I know John do this because he want Ari happy. He like Ari lot. Ari like him lot."

Approaching fifteen (he was born November 25, 1960), John is an outgoing, athletic, fun-loving youngster who alternately resembles Jackie and the Ken-

nedys.* He cannot escape the past. In the winter of
1975, he went on a skiing vacation to the Berkshires
in Massachusetts with his Uncle Ted, Aunt Joan, and
a party of cousins. In a ski lodge, John caught sight of
a portrait of his father on a wall, beneath it was a
plaque. John stopped and said to a friend, "Hey, look
at that." Then he read aloud, "Ask not what your
country can do for you. . . ." John said to his friends,
"That's his most famous quote." Then he turned and
went out into the crisp sunshine.

The day after Jackie and Ari announced their up-
coming wedding, a cartoon appeared in a California
newspaper showing all the Kennedys' including Jackie,
playing touch football. The former First Lady misses
a pass and one of her sisters-in-law says, "Go marry
your Greek! See if we care! We didn't need you and
besides you can't play touch football anyway!"

Funny, yes. Accurate, no. Jackie, a dud at touch
football, may have been banished summarily from a
game—but not from the clan. Not even after she
married Onassis, all rumors notwithstanding.

Countless stories have gone the rounds—many find-
ing their way into print—that Jackie incurred the bitter
and unforgiving enmity of the Kennedy family that
October day when she became Ari's wife. That she
hurt the family. That she tarnished the name of John
F. Kennedy. That she wrecked forever whatever
chances Ted may have had to be elected president.
That they told her, "We don't need you."

---

* Shortly after President Kennedy's death, a visit [by Robbins] to his
ancestral home in County Wexford, Ireland revealed that one of the
very young cousins bore a startling resemblance to John—they could
have been identical twins!

One widely publicized but probably aprocraphyl story was typical of many. Jackie and one of her sisters-in-law were dining in a New York restaurant when the following exchange was supposedly overheard:

Sister-in-law: When are you going to break off with your little Greek?

Jackie: Don't call him that; if you persist, I'll walk out!

Sister-in-law: Think about the family!

Jackie: Family! Family! Always the family! How about thinking of me? (With that, Jackie allegedly stormed out of the restaurant.)

There appears to be little doubt that, from time to time, there has been friction between Jackie and the Kennedys.

She reportedly sometimes refused to take telephone calls from members of the family.

She would "forget" to keep luncheon or dinner dates with them.

She would be unable to hide her boredom with their incessant talk of politics.

She refused to attend the ceremonies officially opening the John F. Kennedy Center for the Performing Arts in Washington in 1971 because Onassis was not invited.

None of this means, however, that there is an ongoing feud or a permanent split. Note:

• Rose Kennedy, the matriarch who sets the tone and direction for the rest of the family, was astonished and perplexed at first, but gave the couple her blessing. "Mother instinctively knows what's right," Eunice Kennedy Shriver has said. "She's rarely in error."

119

• Ted Kennedy sees Jackie often and is always ready to act as friendly adviser. Ted has given orders to the receptionist at his Senate office: "If Mrs. Onassis calls me, put her through immediately, no matter how busy I am."

• She may not be present at all family functions, but she comes to Hyannisport with her children frequently enough on holidays. There are no signs of strain at these family gatherings. On Labor Day, 1971, Ted Kennedy broke up a morning-long interview at Squaw Island just as Jackie drove up with Caroline.

• Pat Lawford and Jean Smith reportedly were opposed to the match. They attended the wedding at the request of Rose, who was unable to come because of the illness of Joe Kennedy. How did John Kennedy's sisters act that day on Skorpios? Coldly proper? Distant? As though they hated the whole thing? Not at all. They giggled, laughed, and had a ball. One American journalist who covered the wedding said, "A long time ago, I learned to spot a phony in this business. And I could tell those two Kennedy girls weren't putting it on. They were genuinely pleased by the wedding.

"One hilarious incident stands out in my mind," the reporter added. "That was a kiss that Jean gave Jackie. Or maybe it was Pat who did it; they were standing so close it was difficult to tell who was who. Somebody jostled Jackie, causing the kiss to land on her chin. The kiss was tried again, but this time a flashbulb went off, and one of them flinched—I'm sure it wasn't Jackie, because that gal really thrives on flashbulbs, whatever she says to the contrary. Anyway, this time the kiss hit the tip of Jackie's left ear. By now the three of them were really amused and burst out laughing. The third kiss was successful."

However, it is true that the marriage announcement

stunned Rose. After years of experience, Rose pays no heed to gossip and rumor; she discounted all the stories linking Jackie to various suitors, if she read them at all. Two problems were of immediate concern to Rose—would the marriage of a Catholic woman to a man of Greek Orthodox faith be valid in the eyes of the Church? And would Caroline and John accept Onassis as a stepfather?

"With contemplation," she wrote in her autobiography, *Times to Remember,* "it seemed to me the first basic fact was that Jackie deserved a full life, a happy future. Jack had been gone five years, thus she had plenty of time to think things over. She was not a person who would jump rashly into anything as important as this, so she must have her own good reasons.

"I decided I ought to put my doubts aside and give Jackie all the emotional support I could in what, as I realized, was bound to be a time of stress for her in the weeks and months ahead. When she called I told her to make her plans as she chose to do, and to go ahead with them with my loving wishes."

After Bobby died, Jackie turned more and more to Ted for counseling. Shortly after the Chappaquiddick affair, and while Ted Kennedy was still being roasted daily by the newspapers, Jackie felt that her personal reassurance of faith would be helpful. She sent the senator a letter saying that since Bobby's death, Caroline was without a Godfather and that it would be so nice if Ted would agree to take his place.

An aide to the senator said, "He was very grateful for the request and readily agreed. He was so pleased to read something other than about Chappaquiddick."

"In her own fashion—she may not show it—Jackie appreciates the concern of the Kennedys," a close friend said. "More than once she confided that she's glad to be part of such a close-knit family. But in all honesty, I have to admit that she also has told me that there are times that she feels that they 'hover about too much.' Those occasions, however, are in the minority, and she has grown to be very fond of the family, especially Rose."

Ari admired Rose enormously. An Onassis cousin offered these revealing glimpses into how Ari felt about her. "A few years ago," the cousin said, "we were having lunch at the roof garden at the King's Palace Hotel on Venizelou Avenue in Athens, when he began speaking about the elder Mrs. Kennedy. He thought she was a very wise woman, and Ari was a man who appreciated wisdom. He told me, 'My admiration for her grows each time I see her. Some people have a special talent to size up a situation very quickly and instinctively do what's right—she is one of those people. Last year when she visited Skorpios, I was very busy in Athens and could only fly home on the weekend. She'd be there, but so were some other people Jackie was entertaining. One of them was the biggest bore that ever lived. This lady talked constantly about her operation. To hear her tell it, she returned from the jaws of death—I think the real reason she did was so that she could continue to bore people.

" 'Rose Kennedy,' he continued, 'sensed how I felt, and the minute I'd find myself cornered by that lady, Mrs. Kennedy came over to rescue me. Even when her back was turned, she seemed to know. I'll always be grateful to her for that!

" 'It was the same way with the children,' Ari said. 'Mrs. Kennedy would just know when they had had enough, and she'd automatically step in. Once Caroline, John, the Radziwill children, and some other young-sters were playing Blind Man's Buff. I believe Anthony

Radziwill was "it," and he was getting tired. That's when Mrs. Kennedy intervened. She invited the entire group to have some iced tea and cookies. They were glad to quit and had been waiting for someone to suggest it. But only Mrs. Kennedy had realized that. She's a wonderful person.' "

For her part, Rose frankly liked Onassis. "He was pleasant, interesting, and, to use a word of Greek origin, charismatic," she says in her book. Interviewed on television late in 1974, shortly before Ari died, she disclosed that Jackie and the children had visited her "a good deal" in her winter home at Palm Beach. "The children come here to swim and lunch," she said. "Ari and I get along quite well. It's one thing to have your mother-in-law visit you, but when you have your wife's ex-mother-in-law, it would be quite formidable. But it's wonderful for me to have this pleasant relationship with him [Ari] so I can see my grandchildren quite comfortably without intruding."

The only time there may have been a misunderstanding occurred on the yacht in the spring of 1969. "Jackie," Ari said, "you wouldn't believe it, but she has locked me out of my own ship!"

Rose Kennedy had come to spend the Easter vacation aboard the *Christina*. The cruise had just begun when the Mediterranean became rough, and Rose retreated to her cabin. When she failed to emerge all day, a concerned Ari looked in on her and found her asleep. After four days of solitude, she finally came out on deck, but she still looked a bit under the weather.

"I hope you're feeling better," Ari said. Then he told her that he had gone in to see her a couple of times.

Rose was shocked. "Do you mean that you actually came into my stateroom?" she demanded.

He admitted that he had. With that, she returned to her room and locked the door. This time no one— not even Ari—could enter to apologize. That evening, however, she emerged in time for dinner, the queasiness apparently gone. As the *meze* (appetizer) was being served, Rose, Jackie, and Ari had a good laugh about the incident.

"Jackie can always look to the Kennedys for firm support," said a friend of the family. "When the clan felt that Jackie might not get a fair share of the Onassis fortune, they stood ready to help.

"After all, Kennedys always help Kennedys!"

CHAPTER XI

A Greek Tragedy

Someday a great dramatist yet unborn, with the skill and insight of a Shakespeare, will seize upon the Jackie and Ari story and create from its elements a great drama. The marriage and the events that surround it shaped up like a Greek tragedy, and seemed headed for the same kind of awesome climax.

All the ingredients of a great play appeared to be present: the marriage of two titans; boundless wealth, family feuds; reported suicides; alleged murder; children anatgonistic to the union. And in the background, the assassination of a head of state and his celebrated family.

That the marriage survived must be counted as a near-miracle, for the roadblocks in its path were monumental.

Consider, first, the attitudes of Onassis' children, which must be weighed heavily because of his deep attachment to them. "It was well known that the Onassis children were disturbed by their father's marriage to Jackie Kennedy," wrote Doris Lilly in *Those Fabulous Greeks*. "They weren't interested in substitute mothers."

Alexander, Ari's first-born, a strangely moody, restless, hot-tempered, hard-living young man, disliked the

125

idea of acquiring Jackie as a stepmother. There is not much doubt in his friends' minds that he opposed the marriage from the start and barely tolerated her afterward.

Reporters noted carefully that Alexander was the last person to enter the Skorpios chapel on the wedding day. "I didn't need a stepmother," he said in a widely quoted statement, "but my father needed a wife." During Ari's courtship of Jackie, Alexander told a friend, "Count on my father to do some pretty weird things. Do you suppose he's getting senile?" (Onassis at the time was earning two hundred thousand dollars a day, he was in his late fifties or early sixties and looked ten years younger. This is hardly evidence of senility!)

Actually, Alexander was so opposed to the marriage he hadn't wanted to come to the ceremony at all, but his father had won him over by striking a bargain. Onassis worried constantly about Alexander's flying. Almost daily, he would plead with the boy to ground himself, fearing that his daring and occasional recklessness would one day result in tragedy. As the wedding day neared, Alexander told Ari yes, he would attend the wedding. But on one condition—his father must from that time on say no more about his flying. Reluctantly, Ari agreed.

Friends disclosed that Alexander was rarely present when Jackie was on Skorpios or in Ari's Paris and London homes. Says one friend, "It was not by accident. He just stayed away."

Once, however, he was at dinner with Jackie on Skorpios when his feelings suddenly surfaced. The talk turned to a chorus girl who had recently married a Greek industrialist. Alexander, who had been drinking, turned to Jackie and said: "You don't think that's so bad, do you—to marry for money." Jackie pretended she hadn't heard. After a brief shocked silence, someone turned to a new subject.

To one of his friends, he confided some intimate thoughts about stepmothers. "When you think your parents are about to get remarried and suddenly another woman steps in, you get all confused and start wondering.

"I really think my mother and father were considering being together again. I don't think I'm being childish or romantic when I say it was about to happen. Everything would have been different if it had worked out that way. But no, I got a new stepmother that I needed as much as I do a bellyache. It's not that I have anything against her personally, but she's just not our type. She goes with orchids and champagne. We mix with garlic and salt water."

Apparently, Alexander's opposition continued long after the marriage. Peter Evans reported in a London newspaper, "He [Alexander] told one of his closest friends, 'I understand my father's fascination for the Kennedy woman. She is beautiful, intelligent, formidable. But maybe she could undermine everything. She could jeopardize a whole epoch.'"

Christina, too, was hardly enchanted by the prospect of acquiring a new mother. Not yet eighteen at the time, she was still the poor little rich girl barely grown up. All accounts picture her as essentially lonely, despite her opulent surroundings, left alone for long periods of time by her globe-trotting father. It requires no penetrating analysis to realize that a young girl in this position would, humanly and understandably, want her daddy to herself, and that the arrival upon the scene of a superbly self-confident, glamorous woman, with whom she scarcely felt able to compete, must have been a threatening experience.

Jackie faced the same problem that other stepparents all over the world have faced in second marriages —how to win over the children. It is never easy. And it wasn't in this case either. Christina, according to reports, was angry, hurt, and resentful. "It was a case of yet another woman taking her mother's place," wrote Willi Frischauer, Onassis' biographer. "They were not tears of joy she shed at the wedding on Skorpios," Frischauer writes in *Millionaire's Islands,* a book published in London. Peter Evans in his article used almost the same words: "Her tears at the Ari-Jackie wedding were blatantly not tears of happiness. She left the celebration with almost indecent speed."

Secretly, friends said, Christina had hoped that Ari would effect a reconciliation with her mother and that she might once again have a semblance of family life. But Ari, dazzled by the president's widow, would not be deterred.

In the early months after the marriage, Christina deliberately and pointedly avoided Jackie. When Jackie was to arrive in Skorpios, Christina would see to it that she was in London. Soon after Jackie left the island, Christina would arrive. They were rarely aboard the yacht at the same time; rarely did they sit down together to a dinner with Onassis.

A family friend reveals, "In the beginning, they just didn't operate on the same wavelength. They tolerated each other and were just barely correct. It was evident that Christina had this ridiculous obsession about Jackie, regarding herself as a clumsy creature when compared to her svelte stepmother."

In July 1971, three years after Jackie and Ari were married, Christina, just twenty, infuriated her father by marrying Joseph Bolker, a Los Angeles real-estate man who was twenty-seven years her senior. Bolker seemed completely out of the Onassis' social circle. (The fact that he was twice her age, divorced, and the father of four children seemed to matter less to Ari than the fact that Bolker was not as rich as Onassis.)

The enraged Ari stopped speaking to his daughter. He ordered his servants: "If my daughter calls, tell her that *I'm in,* but that I do not care to talk to her!" He revised the trust fund he had provided for her—Christina was cut out completely.

Stubborn as her father, Christina went her way; she lived in Los Angeles with her new husband, neither calling nor visiting Ari. On Skorpios, Onassis sulked, muttering about "ungrateful daughters" as he downed the ouzos. Although they were many thousands of miles apart, father and daughter were, emotionally, eyeball to eyeball. And Christina was the one who blinked.

In September, just before her twenty-first birthday and after only five months of marriage, she left for Europe. A few months later, she announced, 'I'm divorcing Joe Bolker for a very simple reason. His work forced him to live in California, and I would have been forced to stay too far from my family. I couldn't bear that."

Once, in a moment of anguish, Ted Kennedy wondered aloud before a nationwide television audience whether some awful curse did actually hang over all the Kennedys. It is frightening that Christina Onassis should have uttered that same agonized cry before her twenty-second birthday.

Tragedy upon tragedy entered her young life, as

129

well as the life of her famous father. These terrible blows that fell must surely have had a profound effect upon her, upon Onassis, and upon his marriage to Jackie.

Now we must meet handsome, suave Stavros Niarchos, Ari's archrival in business and love. Niarchos, born in 1909, is a rich and powerful shipping magnate who had been feuding with Onassis since the 1930s. The two played a continual game of oneupmanship that was almost amusing. If one day Onassis added another tanker to his fleet, Niarchos purchased an addition to *his* fleet the following day. Ari bought Skorpios— and Niarchos purchased the island of Spetsopoula. Ari bought the yatch *Christina;* Niarchos acquired the *Creole.* Ari bought an El Greco; so did Niarchos.

Onassis married Tina Livanos in 1946, and the following year, Niarchos wed Tina's sister Eugenie. In 1965, Niarchos divorced Eugenie to marry Charlotte Ford, twenty-four-year-old daughter of Henry Ford II. Three years afterward, Onassis took unto himself an even more famous woman as bride—Jackie!

Niarchos' marriage to Charlotte Ford lasted fourteen months, after which Niarchos took up again with Eugenie where they had left off, with the explanation that it wasn't necessary to remarry because the marriage to Charlotte had been formally dissolved and therefore had never existed.

On May 3, 1970, on Spetospoula, a two-hundred-forty-acre island in the Aegean a short distance from Piraeus, Eugenie, only forty-two years old, died, apparently from an overdose of sleeping pills. Willi Frischauer writes in *Millionaire's Islands* that she and Niarchos had quarreled that night and that Eugenie went upstairs "to find release from her misery in sleep." She took two Seconal tablets, he says, "her usual dose," but sleep would not come. She went downstairs, where the quarrel began anew, and once again Eugenie returned to her bedroom. "Again she reached for the Seconal bottle—and swallowed the lot, some forty tablets," Frischauer writes.

Subsequently, an autopsy disclosed bruises on Eugenie's abdomen, neck, eye, and temple. The Office of the Public Prosecutor of Piraeus sought to show before an investigating magistrate that the injuries, fourteen in all, resulted from kicks and blows from fists. The magistrate appointed a group of eight experts, including doctors, surgeons, pharmacologists, and chemists, to study the findings. After evaluating the evidence, the committee concluded that the bodily injuries were "slight" and had not contributed to Eugenie's death.

A year after Eugenie's death, Niarchos married Ari's former wife, Tina, in a simple ceremony. Ari was furious. His sole motive, Onassis fumed, was spite. However, *Der Spiegel,* a widely circulated German publication, suggested another reason, a practical one —"It's assumed in Athens," *Der Spiegel* declared in an article, "that Niarchos only entered the marriage with Tina to protect property. About two-thirds of her fortune belonged to the estate of the late Eugenie."

And then, with terrifying suddenness, tragedy struck again.

On Monday, January 22, 1973, Alexander took off from the Athens airport in a twin-engine amphibian Piaggio piloted by Donald McCusker, a forty-eight-year-old American from Westerville, Ohio. Alexander was trying out McCusker for his fleet of air taxis. Also aboard was Donald McGregor, a fifty-eight-year-old pilot whom McCusker was to replace. Shortly after it was airborne, the plane nosed down and crashed.

Alexander was pulled unconscious from the wreckage and rushed to a hospital, where he was placed under intensive care. Onassis and Jackie, in New York, rushed to Athens with a leading Boston surgeon. Alexander's face had been smashed beyond recognition; even if he survived, he would be a living vegetable. On Tuesday, he succumbed to a brain hemorrhage. At his bedside were Tina, Ari, Jackie, and Christina. The two other occupants of the plane were injured, but recovered.

Later, Onassis charged that the plane had been sabotaged by enemies seeking to strike at him through his son. He offered a one-million-dollar reward to anyone who could provide leads. Onassis believed to the end of his life that his son had been murdered in a calculated effort to destroy his empire. However, no proof has ever turned up.

Alexander's death crushed Onassis. Never again would he regain his zest for life. Says one friend, "Suddenly, the man seemed to crumple. The joy went out of life. It showed in his face, his eyes, the way he walked. It was sad, so sad. Looking at him, I found it hard to hold back the tears."

Onassis' reaction at the loss of his son recalls the grief of Joseph P. Kennedy, patriarch of the Kennedy clan, after his oldest son, Joseph, was killed in a plane crash over the English Channel during World War II. Kennedy, whose career was often compared to that of Onassis, shut himself in his room for weeks, weeping and listening to symphonic music. Onassis, too, neglected his business, spoke to few people, and wept for days—sometimes convulsively.

"Ari suffered a deep wound when his son died," a *Christina* crew member said. "He used to go to his grave often and spend hours there—always at night. I don't think he wanted anyone to see him cry—darkness covered up the tears."

Another blow came not long after.

On October 11, 1974, a Friday, Onassis' former wife Tina, now married to his archfoe Niarchos, was found dead in her lavish Paris apartment. At once, mystery surrounded her death. A spokesman at the London headquarters of Niarchos' firm said a blood clot in Tina's leg had broken off, moved up to her heart, and blocked blood circulation. From Paris came a statement from Tina's secretary attributing the death to a "heart attack" or a "lung edema." Two French sources—*France-Soir,* an afternoon newspaper, and Agence-France-Presse speculated that Tina may have succumbed to an overdose of sleeping pills.

A tearful Christina, who heard the news while visiting in the United States, flew at once to Paris. An autopsy report found no trace of violence. Later, pathologists said Tina had died of natural causes.

Tina was buried in Lausanne, Switzerland, beside her sister. Onassis did not attend the funeral. Christina, red-eyed, weeping bitterly, watched as her mother's body was lowered into its grave. She said not a word to Niarchos, who stood a short distance from her.

The effects of these tragedies upon the girl Christina can only be guessed; yet one can surely assume that they must have been profound.

Christina cannot have been too happy at this time, for just two months before her mother's death, she had been rushed to Middlesex Hospital, London, and registered under an assumed name—C. Dania. She had remained there a little less than a week. Subsequently, Niarchos had stated publicly that she had tried to take her own life with a "massive overdose of sleeping pills." (This was reported in the press but was later denied by her family and others.)

Could a marriage—any marriage—withstand such onslaughts? Little wonder that, afterward, Mrs. Hugh Auchincloss, Jackie's mother, was to say, "They had their difficult moments, but there was never any question of divorce." Or that Christina herself would admit there were "problems." Christina Cafarakis, former purser aboard the *Christina* who revealed the existence of the prenuptial contract, wrote in his book, *The Fabulous Onassis,* that there was no doubt that Onassis had decided to get a divorce and *The New York Times* was to say, later, "Rumors of a divorce between Mr. and Mrs. Onassis existed, although they were always denied."

Close friends felt that neither Jackie nor Ari appeared happy in the latter years of the marriage. One of Jackie's friends, the wife of a retired corporate executive who had described how pleased Jackie had seemed to be a few years before, visited her on Skorpios again in 1973. She said, "The change was like day to night. She seemed apprehensive about the future. I don't think she mentioned Greece at all. She seemed to be in one black mood after the other. Young John was away at the time, but Caroline was there. Once Caroline asked if she could borrow something. I don't remember what it was, but it was something simple like a sweater or a scarf. Jackie got indignant and spoke sharply to the poor child. A short time later Jackie apologized, but it was obvious that she wasn't feeling top hole. While I was there, Jackie gave one of her lavish parties. She stocked up on exotic foods, champagne, and hired musicians. She invited dozens of guests, and after they arrived, she just disappeared into her room. Ari was in New York at the time, but that wasn't the reason. She just didn't seem to care."

As for Ari in 1973, the following vignette tells a poignant story. A friend who had known him for more than thirty years revealed that not long after Alexander's death he came upon the shipping magnate sitting alone at a sidewalk café in Athens.

"Ari could hold his liquor," the friend said, "but it was obvious that he had been drinking heavily. I was with some people, and I told them to go on and that I would catch up with them later. I sat down next to Ari. At first he was silent, which wasn't like him.

"After a while, he began to talk. He talked about his boy. Slowly, softly, he spoke about Alexander—how much he loved him, how he missed him. He said that other than Christina, he was all alone—Jackie just refused to understand him.

"For half an hour, he continued to speak in that same sad way. Then I offered to take him home, but he said all he wanted was a taxi. I was pleased to see that he walked out in a straight fashion. He didn't seem drunk anymore.

"I guess he got home all right, because I saw him at a dinner party several days later. The episode wasn't mentioned—he was there with Jackie.

"But I will never forget the sight of the man sitting there, so alone and so very sad."

CHAPTER XII

Alexander the *Ainigma*

● "A bland, unfeeling, humorless youth who insists on having his own way whether right or wrong. He knows but one thing—how to spend money he never earned."—*A former Greek Army officer who participated in the 1967 purge*

● "When I accompanied him to the Orient to meet with important Japanese industrialists, I was very impressed with his shrewd mind for high finances, and he made me feel that when he eventually took the business over it would be in good hands."—*Nigel Neilson, Onassis' chief spokesman and liaison man in the British Isles*

● "He was the Number One playboy of the western world, a typical product of the very rich. All he cared about was fast cars, fast planes, and fast women."—*From a Polish radio newscast*

● "He was dedicated and unassuming and was concerned with helping people. Thousands upon thousands of poor Greek islanders mourned his untimely death."—*Helen Speronis, public-relations executive in the Athens office of Olympic Airways*

All of these widely disparate statements were made about one man—Ari's only son, Alexander Onassis, who died tragically at the age of twenty-four on January 23, 1973, twenty-seven hours after his plane crashed at the Athens airport.

Which of them most accurately describes young Onassis? The obituaries told little—only that he was born on April 30, 1948, in Harkness Pavilion, New York City, that he was christened Alexander in memory of his father's uncle who was hanged by the Turks after the sack of Smyrna, and that he was reared in incredible luxury. He was five feet seven inches tall, with close-cropped black hair, thick lips, heavy-lidded eyes, and a strong, jutting chin. He went to school in Paris and Switzerland and studied economics for a brief time in London, dropping out to indulge his passion for speed and women. Not much more.

Young as he was, Alexander, almost totally unknown to Americans, was a complex human being. One former girl friend, Stephanie Pappas, a dark-haired, extremely attractive model in her middle thirties, said, "He was like a jigsaw puzzle. You had to fit together all the pieces to understand him." One of his closest friends, twenty-seven-year-old Nikolas Danos, said, "He was an *ainigma*—an enigma—but a stimulating one. It was hard to figure him out."

Clearly, his parents' divorce, which took place when Alexander was barely thirteen, left a scar. A woman relative who lives near the Onassis villa in Glyfada reveals, "One day young Alexandros came into my house and ran into my skirts. He sobbed, 'They don't love me. They fight all the time.' "

"Divorce inevitably involves rupture and loss," writes psychologist Allan Fromme. "Although it is possible to help a child overcome the difficulties of growing up in a broken home, it warrants serious effort on the part of the guardian parent. It's when the divorce occurs anywhere between the child's third and twelfth year that he will be most sensitive to its effects."

Apparently Ari was too busy to make the serious effort. His response to Alexander's confusion and fears was to increase his already high allowance and to buy him a gasoline-powered toy automobile. Nikolas Danos says, "Alexander would talk about that time in his life often. He used to say that if he ever had children he would never expose them to divorce. 'It does something to your insides,' he'd say. 'Grinds them up into little pieces and then spits them out!' "

Danos has been a tennis pro, lifeguard, and ditch-digger. On two different occasions he has traveled around the world. "When I need money, I work," he says. He met Alexander while he was parking cars in Monte Carlo. He admired Alexander's Ferrari and the two struck up a friendship. Danos says, "Alexander would abruptly change the subject. Once we were sitting in an outdoor café in the Plaka and making comments on 'asses' that walked by. He was an expert on asses. He liked them round but firm. He particularly liked the ass on the waitress that served our table. He ordered a lot of things that he had no intention of eating just to watch her walk away from the table. . . . She'd shake it real nice.

"But then suddenly he got real serious again. He was often like that. That time he asked me, 'Do you know how many people go to bed hungry each night?' I said I didn't know, and he replied, "Millions!' Then he returned to judging asses. I tell you that he was an *ainigma!*"

Ms. Pappas adds to the picture.

"When Alexander would come to see me, he'd always bring some expensive present, but he didn't make you feel cheap. It was as if you were doing him a great favor in accepting it. He'd sit in my apartment on my oak rocking chair and talk about his childhood. I remember he'd tell me that sometimes his father would put him to sleep by singing him a song about the sea. I could tell by the way Alexander was telling it that he had liked it tremendously, but that it hadn't happened very often. He'd also tell me that he was named half after his dead great-uncle and also after Alexander the Great. 'So guess what that makes me?' he'd say."

Before his death, Alexander lived on the tenth floor of the Athens Hilton Hotel. "He was very kind and considerate to the personnel," said manager Jean Pierre Piquet. "Although he was still a young boy, he didn't have any *Playboy* magazines in his room, only copies of *Aviation* and *Flying*. He had lots of books on that subject in many languages. He spoke English, French, Italian, and Greek. I was very glad to have him as a guest in the hotel."

A clerk in the hotel added, "Alexander could see that I was worried about something, and he asked me what it was. I told him that my wife was sick and needed an operation. Without asking me any further questions he gave me fifteen thousand drachmas [about five hundred dollars]. I thanked him and said that I would pay it back. He joked and said, 'Okay, when you're as rich as me.' He didn't make it hard to accept the money. Do you know what I mean?

"I could tell when he made out well with a lady. He would hum a funny-sounding tune that gave me the tip-off. It sounded like the opening bars they used to play for victory in the war.* When he didn't hum that song, then I'd know that the evening wasn't so good.

"But I'd say that most of the time he made out fine. When he was finished with a lady, that was that. But

---

* The theme from Beethoven's Fifth Symphony.

one woman refused to believe it—she'd come around the hotel and wait for him for hours to come through the lobby, but everybody who worked there liked Alexander and would smuggle him out through the employee's exit."

After countless interludes, all instantly forgotten, Alexander seemed to have discovered the real thing in Fiona von Thyssen, the former Fiona Campbell-Walter. She had been a well-known British model and was the former wife of a German industrialist, Count Heinrich von Thyssen. She and her children lived in St. Moritz, where Alexander spent much of his time. He told his father that he wanted to marry Fiona, who was fifteen years his senior. Ari was opposed to the match and tried to break it up, but Alexander remained firm, and the Fiona affair lasted for many years. Ari remarked to a crony, "When I was Alexander's age, I would have acted the same way. The boy's got spunk!"

Meanwhile, Ari kept giving his son more and more responsibility. He had Alexander accompany him on important business trips. He sent him to Japan to negotiate a multimillion-dollar deal. Alexander had always been interested in flying and after amassing one thousand hours of soloing, Ari put him in charge of Olympic Airways' island service. Combining his knowledge of planes with his father's business acumen, Alexander turned the venture into a profitable enterprise and made it possible for isolated islands to be linked to the mainland.

One of them, Kithira, located off the southernmost tip of the Mani peninsula, went into deep mourning when he died, as though each native had lost a birthright son. Alexander had personally rallied the inhabitants to build an airport with a four-thousand-foot runway. The air link had made the islanders prosper. Said a Kithira fisherman, "Alexander Onassis gave us our manhood. It was a sad day to learn that his has ended. He will remain forever in our hearts."

Alexander's friends are a vigorous bunch. One young man, a husky twenty-seven-year-old professional soccer player, said that he had met Alexander in Athens after an all-night party. Both were bored and left together for a local bar.

"I wouldn't call Alexander a playboy," he said. "I think of a playboy with only one thing in mind— pussy. It wasn't that way with him. Oh, sure, he would talk about it plenty. And not only talk, action too. But he'd brood a lot too, about his life and his family.

"He loved his father, of course, but I wonder if he completely admired him. Yes, he was proud of the man's fantastic accomplishments in the business world, and I would often feel he wanted to be like him. But then he would sit quietly, a funny look on his face, and he'd say to me: 'There's only one Aristotle Socrates Onassis—thank God!'

"It was his sister, Christina, he really cared about. He'd talk about her and his face would light up—he didn't want anybody to bother her. Once I made some remark that Alexander felt was improper to his sister. Even though she wasn't present, I had to apologize. I rose and, pretending she was present, I told her I was sorry.

"He was easy-going until he got drunk, and then no matter what you did or said, he'd refuse to move. He was sure stubborn, and drink made him even more so. He was pretty strong, and he'd make himself rigid and dare you to budge him. It was very difficult to do!

"I was with him shortly after he learned that his mother was going to marry Stavros Niarchos. He sure drank that night and yelled out loud, 'My uncle will

soon become my stepfather! Did everybody hear that?
My uncle will soon become my stepfather! Stepfather!
Stepfather!'

"He just sat and stared. Didn't look to the right or to
the left. He just sat and drank.

"He was a strange one, that fellow."

CHAPTER XIII

The King Is Dead

Life changed dramatically for Onassis in 1973, after Alexander was killed. Suddenly he ceased to enjoy all business transactions and became forgetful, quarrelsome, and illogical.

In London, an executive for a large British petrol company who insisted on anonymity said, "I can't say that I always cherished meeting with Mr. Onassis—what with his constantly striking a sharp bargain that somehow managed to favor him. But on the last few occasions that we met, I actually found myself feeling sorry for him. He would completely disregard what he had come for and talk about his early days. Often, he would just sit and nod; when he wasn't nodding, he would insist on some impossible terms and contradict himself. If I hadn't known better, I'd have classified him as senile or bewitched!"

Vassilios Mavros, a fifteen-year-old shoeshine boy who operates in Athens' Syngrou Square near the Olympic Airways office, said, "I shine his shoes lots of time. The last time I shine him he yell for me to work faster. So I speed up. When over, he pays for shine but no tip. Before, he always be first-rate and always big tips. I figure something's wrong."

Something was indeed wrong.

145

Onassis had been told that he was suffering from a rare debilitating neuromuscular disease of unknown origin, myasthenia gravis. Doctors know little about the illness, except that it is a metabolic disorder—a defect in the chemical process preventing transmission of impulses at the point where the nerves and muscles meet. The most frequent initial sign is weakness of the eye muscles. Afterward, there can be difficulty in swallowing and abnormal fatigue.*

Ari had to tape his eyelids to keep them from drooping. He wore dark glasses to hide the tape, but although no announcement was made, the secret soon came out. In the fall of 1974, Onassis entered a New York hospital for a week of treatment, but it was determined that little could be done for him. Ari knew that death would come soon. Ordinarily he was a great fighter, but this time he didn't put up any resistance.

On February 6, Jackie bundled him into an Olympic Airways jet especially outfitted with medical equipment, and he was flown to Paris. He spent the night in his penthouse apartment near the Arc de Triomphe and was then driven to the nearby American Hospital in Neuilly-sur-Seine. (The hospital was opened in 1910 by a group of American businessmen to care for American citizens living or traveling abroad and it has a splendid medical reputation.) Ari was placed in Room 217 of the Eisenhower Wing.

Two days after he was admitted, Ari underwent surgery for removal of his gall bladder. Although the operation was successful, a heavy influenza set in, and he was kept in the hospital for five weeks.

An English newspaper reported that a young French

---

* The *Merck Manual of Diagnosis and Therapy*, a physician's reference book, says, "Some cases are rapidly fatal, due to respiratory failure or aspiration; in others the life span is little affected."

nurse, Francoise Picquel, who had been assigned to help care for Onassis, said, "Only his closest family were allowed to visit him. Christina came every day and spent hours at her father's side, often in silence. Sometimes his wife, Jackie, would sit in a chair at the other side of the bed. The two women never spoke to each other.

"Onassis spoke to his daughter in Greek, to Jackie in English, and to me in French. At night sometimes he would take my hand and rub it against his cheek. In this simple gesture, I could read all his gratitude."

There were periods when Ari seemed to be making progress, and, according to intimates of Jackie's, the doctors told the former First Lady that she could safely leave her husband's bedside for a few days and fly to New York. She wanted to come to the United States to view the television documentary Caroline had worked on. Jackie had been shuttling between the two cities in previous weeks.

She arrived in New York on Thursday evening. An aide in the Fifth Avenue apartment said, "She had telephoned the hospital on Friday night and had been given no cause for alarm."

But on Saturday, March 15, the telephone rang. The call was from Neuilly-sur-Seine. Ari was dead.

Dr. Maurice Mercadier, one of the physicians who had been treating Onassis, said death was due to bronchial pneumonia, which "resisted all antibiotics." Ari had been receiving cortisone, which, the doctor said, had lowered his resistance to infection and made the pneumonia "uncontrollable."

At 6:07 P.M. Jackie, wearing dark glasses, a black leather coat, a black turtleneck sweater, black stockings, and black shoes, emerged from her apartment building and was immediately surrounded by more than a hundred people who had heard the news on television or radio. While reporters and photographers tried to intercept her, Secret Service men and New York City police escorted Jackie to a waiting limousine. She was driven to Kennedy Airport, where she took Air France Flight 070 to Paris.

The next morning, at 7 A.M., she arrived at Charles de Gaulle Airport and went directly to the Onassis apartment on Avenue Foch. Ari had asked for a simple funeral. A *Christina* crew member reported that he had once overheard a conversation Onassis had with Churchill about death. Churchill had said, "Death won't strike you for a long time. As for me, I fear death will come soon. I have it all planned out." Then he spoke of his grandiose burial plans. Ari told him that he wanted something simple. "But it's your very last act on earth," replied the former prime minister. "They will expect a superior show. I say give it to them."

Ari hadn't been convinced and had told Jackie many times he desired simplicity. She had agreed to honor his wish. At 5:15 P.M., still in the black leather coat, she was driven to the hospital, where she was told that her husband's body was in the chapel. Walking alone, she pushed open the chapel's bronze doors behind which the body was lying on a bier with a Greek Orthodox icon on its chest.

A hospital attendant said that when Jackie emerged some minutes later she was white-faced and stumbled as she was helped into the waiting car. "She seemed like any other grieving wife who has just seen her dead husband," he said.

Jackie returned to the apartment at Avenue Foch and remained secluded until she departed for Skorpios.

Again a large crowd gathered outside the house, and one woman, asked by a reporter why she was here, replied, "I want to see close-up what the widow of two of the most important men of the century looks like."

Hundreds of messages arrived, among them a telegram from Greek Prime Minister Constantine Karamanlis. He told reporters, "Mr. Aristotle Onassis was a personality recognized internationally in the sector of enterprising activities. For this reason, his death has caused a sensation, in Greece and all over the world."

Archbishop Meletos, the Greek Orthodox Metropolitan of France, visited the hospital chapel and prayed over the body. A group of Greek tourists gathered outside the hospital and conducted a brief service that included the singing of hymns.

Costa Conialides, an Onassis cousin, had been assigned the task of arranging for the funeral—he knew that Ari wanted to be buried next to Alexander and that he wanted the entire ceremony to be natural and unaffected. Under Greek Orthodox church law, no one may be buried inside a church but adjacent wings to the building may be built to cover tombs. Ari was aware of that when he planned Alexander's funeral and had approved plans for his own tomb. He had given his gardener instructions that two tall cypress trees were not to be touched.

On March 18, Ari's body was placed in a plain oak coffin and flown to Actium near the Greek port of Preveza, on the Ionian Sea. Jackie, Christina, Ted Kennedy, and Ari's three sisters were also in the plane. Jackie was the first to disembark and seemed to be supporting Christina, who followed close behind. According to the London *Daily Telegraph,* Christina seemed near tears and asked, "Why are all these people around us? Get them away."

Jackie replied, "Take it easy now. It will soon be over!"

Caroline and John had arrived earlier at Actium airport with their grandmother, Mrs. Auchincloss. A cortege of cars then drove them to Nidri; from there they could make the two-mile crossing to Skorpios. The coffin was placed in a cabin cruiser, and the immediate family took a second launch. The rest of the mourners made the trip by ferry. Helicopters whirred overhead carrying television crews.

When the funeral party landed in Skorpios, the coffin was unloaded and the mourners fell in behind it. The solemn procession walked up the hill, the chapel bell tolling slowly. Jackie clasped her son's arm, and Caroline walked with her uncle. In the distance was the *Christina,* its flag at half-mast. Outside the chapel were a half-dozen wreaths on white tripods. A large one of pink hyacinths, pink and white carnations, and white lilies bore the message, "To Ari from Jackie." The chapel courtyard was lined with hundreds of white lilies, their pots draped in red velvet.

Only part of the fifty invited mourners were able to crowd into the chapel to hear the brief funeral service. There was no eulogy. In keeping with Ari's desire for simplicity, the ceremony was conducted by Father Apostolous Savitzanos, the village priest of Nidri. He read St. Paul's Epistle to the Thessalonians. Then he intoned, "Come and give him your last kiss," and, according to Greek Orthodox tradition, each mourner kissed an icon placed on the coffin lid. Jackie, her children, and Ted Kennedy also crossed themselves.

The coffin was then carried outside and placed on the sarcophagus. The mourners followed Father Savitzanos, who was intoning prayers. Then the coffin was lowered into the concrete vault. Christina, shaking with sobs, stood at the head of the grave. After the final prayer, she threw in one handful of dirt.

Jackie decided to stay overnight on the island, but most of the mourners were ferried to Nidri and then departed for Athens. They were closely observed by Nidri natives. An old man who appeared to be in his late eighties told us, "They were mostly very quiet, but a lady, who must be a relative, said to another lady that it was too bad that the good died young, and then she looked right at me. Ari wasn't so very young, and I can't help it if I'm still alive!"

Another man said, "The people who came for Ari's funeral were almost like army soldiers the way they walked to the ferry. The only thing different from the army was the way they were dressed and that there were ladies there."

A woman whose daughter works on Skorpios said, "Jackie's shock hasn't come yet—it's after the death that you really know about it. The next morning, Jackie paid an early morning visit to Ari's grave. Then she, her mother, and her children left the island to board a plane for Paris.

Once again Jacqueline Bouvier Kennedy Onassis was a widow, with the eyes of the world upon her.

CHAPTER XIV

The Money

With Onassis' death, had Jackie become one of the world's richest women? Rarely has there been as much speculation about an individual's financial worth as there was when Ari died. Rumors bounced around the world and found their way into the press, each more fanciful than the next. One said Ari had left his widow two hundred million dollars and her children twenty million dollars each. Presumably, this was based on the assumption that, under Greek law, a widow is entitled to one-eighth of her husband's estate. The flaw in the reasoning, however, was that most of Onassis' holdings were registered in other countries. On April 12, *The New York Times* reported in a front-page story that Jackie would receive three million dollars in the will. Citing as sources friends of the Onassis family, the story also said that one million dollars in trust funds would be set up for each of Jackie's children. *Time* magazine reported, "The best guess is that Jackie will end up with about $100 million, and her children, Caroline and John, with $15 million each."

They were all wrong.

How much was Ari really worth? He had spread his holdings throughout the world, and it was difficult to determine his actual worth, because it was so tangled. His financial arrangements were so complex that only he could understand them.*

Seatrade, a highly respected British shipping journal, recently published an estimate made by Wall Street and Swiss sources. (*Seatrade* won't vouch for any of the figures.) The report implied that Onassis had a controlling interest (a third or more) in seventy companies in the United States, Western Europe, Latin America, and the Middle East. The companies engaged in shipping, tourism, real estate, and industrial activities. The total of the holdings was placed at nine hundred million dollars, but when their mortgages were subtracted, the value dropped to five hundred million dollars.** Less conservative appraisals put the Onassis financial empire at a round billion dollars.

An Onassis competitor who was lunching at the National Yacht Club recently said, "Ari was a great one for secrecy—he wouldn't let his left hand know what his right hand was doing. Everything he did was a big secret—I don't think his heirs will ever know what they really possess. Several years ago I put in a new swimming pool, and I remembered how clean and pure the water was in the *Christina* pool. So I asked Ari what kind of filter he had. He was about to tell me, but he suddenly drew back and said that he didn't recall. It was just a case of his not giving away any information—call it force of habit.

"Perhaps that's why he was so successful. You know that nearly every one of his tankers was a separate

* International bankers say that large sums of money will probably go unclaimed, because Onassis had safe deposit boxes throughout the world, and only he personally knew where they were located.

** Just as the popular press often exaggerated the Onassis wealth, many financial experts tend to write down his assets.

entity—a different company. He kept everything apart."

It's almost an impossible task to give an accurate breakdown on how many ships he owned. Several years ago, *U.S. News and World Report* tried.

- Fifty-three vessels were listed as owned by Panamanian companies and sailed under the Liberian flag.
- Nine belonged to a Liberian firm and used the Liberian flag.
- Twelve were owned by Victory Carriers, Inc., of the United States and sailed under the American flag.
- One vessel sailing under the Greek flag was owned by a Panamanian company.
- One was under both a Panamanian company and the Panamanian flag.

The experts who compiled the list said it was probable that Onassis owned many more ships. He had vessels built in the United States, West Germany, Japan, and elsewhere. Japanese sources said that twelve ships, totaling over eight hundred thousand gross tons, were on order in that country.

Whenever Ari was informed of a financial list that reported his holdings, he'd have a stock answer—"It could be accurate, but on the other hand, it's probably not." Even his last will and testament remained a deep secret until it was published in Athens on June 6.

On June 3, 1974, Aristotle Onassis took off from Acapulco in his Lear jet, bound for New York. Shortly after he was airborne, he drew a gold pen from his inside jacket pocket and began writing on a pad of legal-sized paper in a stilted schoolboy hand "My Will."

For almost six hours, he continued writing, stopping only for a quick meal; and when the jet landed at La-Guardia Airport, his last will and testament, covering eighteen pages, was completed.

Few outside the Onassis family knew the will existed. After his death, one of his biographers wrote about reports that Ari had drawn up a "new will" aboard a plane. "I doubt this report," he said, "and suspect that it is merely an attempt to embarrass Ari's widow or to keep her from going to court."

The will was real, and it astonished the world.

For one thing, Onassis, never socially conscious to a significant degree in his lifetime, left half his vast fortune to charity. He left instructions to establish a philanthropic foundation that would create or support public welfare institutions, mostly in Greece. The foundation was to be set up in Vaduz, Lichtenstein (which has no income taxes) in the name of his dead son, Alexander, and would be administered by a board of directors that would include Christina and Jacqueline.

For another, the will spelled out precisely what Jackie would receive. Ari left her an annual inflation-proof allowance of two hundred fifty thousand dollars, consisting of one hundred thousand dollars a year from tax-free bonds, an additional hundred thousand a year in personal income, and fifty thousand dollars a year for her children, also tax free. (When they reach twenty-one, that sum will go to Jackie.) Onassis made provisions in the will for this sum to be readjusted every three years for inflation, "so that their buying value [will] stay as much as possible at the level of the buying value of the year 1973."

Ari disclosed in his will that Jackie had signed and sworn to an agreement renouncing her hereditary rights to any part of his estate in return for the allowance. Onassis stressed that if Jackie contests the will in court, he "commands" his executors and the rest of his heirs to fight the action "through all legal means," with his estate bearing the costs.

Thus Ari at long last admitted after his death that a prenuptial pact had indeed existed, a fact he had vehemently denied earlier.

When it was reported in 1968 that he and Jackie had signed a premarriage contract containing one hundred seventy clauses, Ari snapped, "Not a bit of truth in it!" Jackie's personal secretary, Nancy Tuckerman, also protested the story. "That's ridiculous," she said. "Honestly, there's no such thing. It's really quite unfair and unkind. It's so fabricated."

The written transaction was supposed to include the following clauses.

- Separate bedrooms for Jackie and Ari were mandatory.
- Jackie was not required to bear Ari a child.
- The couple agreed to spend only holidays and summer vacations together.
- If Ari decided to walk out of the marriage, he had to give Jackie ten million dollars for each year they had been wed.
- If Jackie left Ari before five years of marriage were completed, she would only receive a lump sum of twenty million dollars.
- Jackie was to receive an annual allowance amounting to about four hundred fifty thousand dollars a year for herself and the children.

A prominent Greek attorney who practices in Athens explained that it was not uncommon to draw up such an agreement. "Many brides insist on it," said the tall, erect lawyer, who is also a law professor at Athens University. "A premarriage contract has long been part of Greek culture," he added. "There is even a provision for one in Greek Orthodox Church law. It is especially used by the very rich, who want to list valuable possessions that are too numerous to be trusted to memory."

There have been many rumors, all citing "reliable" sources, but the plain truth is that, despite all the speculation, no outsiders really know how much money Jackie actually received under her prenuptial agreement. Columnist Jack Anderson (and others) have said that under the pact, Onassis handed over three million dollars to Jackie in tax-free bonds. He was also reported to have set up one-million-dollar trust funds for each of the children.

The rest of Ari's estate went to Christina, who also received in addition an inflation-proof annuity of two hundred fifty thousand dollars. Christina, then, actually inherited the shipping empire. A few days after her father's funeral, she took charge, telling company executives in London, "Although I may be a woman, I am an Onassis. From now on, if there is anything to discuss or to be decided, you will be dealing with me."

What about the luxurious yacht, *Christina,* and the island kingdom of Skorpios?

Jackie received one-quarter of the fabulous yacht, his daughter three-quarters. However, operating the ship costs five hundred thousand dollars a year. If the two women find they are unable or unwilling to keep it going, Onassis stipulated, they may remove all valuable object, including the El Grecos, replace them with

copies, and offer the yacht to the Greek government
for use by the head of state.

Ari bequeathed Skorpios to "the personal use" of
his wife and daughter, provided they could maintain
the island at one hundred thousand dollars a year.
Otherwise, it would go to Greece for use as a presidential summer residence. If the government does not
accept it, the island will be given to Olympic Airways
as a summer camp for families of the airline's employees. In a touching gesture, Ari excluded from the gift
the chapel and tomb of his son.

When a copy of Onassis' will was obtained and
translated, it was revealed that Ari, who had had
limited schooling, had absorbed the business and legal
know-how to prepare a thoroughly detailed legal in-
strument disposing of his great wealth precisely as he
wished. The text of the will appears at the end of this
book.

CHAPTER XV

Long Live Queen Christina

The scene—Athens Airport in the bright sunlight of a day in early June 1975.

She flew in aboard her private jet. She strode through the doors at one end of the large rectangular lounge, still in mourning for her father—she wore a simple black dress and black stockings; a small black bag clutched in her hand. She wore no makeup and no jewelry except for tiny pearl earrings glimpsed beneath her hair, which was tied in a pony tail.

Her eyes, dark brown and piercing, took in the lounge in a quick glance. To her left, a bar, jammed two deep. To her right, the large board flashing arrivals and departures. In front, imitation leather chairs where travelers waited for their planes. A few looked up as she went by, no recognition in their faces.

Six waiting newsmen converged upon her.

Christina Onassis, one of the world's richest women, perhaps the richest of all, was returning to Athens shortly after the death of her father.

She was intercepted in her advance across the lounge. She paused, surprised. Three men accompanying her moved forward quickly, then stopped when they spotted the pads and pencils of journalists. Flashbulbs popped.

Christina, in person, is far lovelier than her pictures indicate. She is one of those individuals (Wallis Windsor is another) who do not photograph well. Those who have pegged her as unattractive are totally wrong.

She is five feet five inches tall and weighs about one hundred twenty well-proportioned pounds. Her skin, dark like her father's, is clear and glows with health. She has an oval face, white, even, large teeth, a graceful chin, and a radiant smile. Her small nose, once bulbous like Ari's, has been shortened and shaped by plastic surgery.

She is inclined to stockiness. At other times, she has appeared distinctly heavy, thanks to a fondness for cheeseburgers. But in June, she had slimmed down to a trim figure. Her bust is medium-sized, her legs are well-proportioned, her hips well-curved. "I'm still in mourning for my father," she told reporters on this occasion. "I hope I can be worthy of him." Then she turned and walked rapidly from the lounge, out into the hot Grecian sun.

Christina had all the advantages money could buy. Born December 11, 1950, she grew up in almost unbelievable splendor. But she had very little else—her father was busy increasing his fortune, and her mother was occupied with being a jet-setter. Newspapers started calling Christina "the poor little rich girl."

She was guarded closely by governesses, servants, and nurses. Christina and her brother, Alexander, were shuttled from the plush penthouse apartment in Paris, to the luxurious yacht that lay off Monte Carlo, to the magnificent villa in Glyfada. When she was nine, her parents were divorced and another home was added— her mother's elegant mansion in Nassau. All the domiciles were supersplendid, but impersonal.

Ari adored his daughter—he called her "Chrysomous" (My Golden One)—but he could find little time for her. This aspect of their relationship was poignantly illustrated by a story told by a family friend.

"One day, Ari and I were in his Monte Carlo office discussing business. Without a warning, he jumped up from his desk and said that he wanted to buy Christina a present. He told me that it wasn't her birthday, but he just remembered that he had promised to go home that evening, and he had to leave for Argentina instead. So he had his chauffeur drive us to a toy store. He wasn't looking for an ordinary present like you and I might buy for our daughters, but something extraspecial. He asked for the most expensive item they had. The saleslady brought out a dainty ballerina doll that, when wound, danced to the tune of the 'Sugar Plum Fairy.' It cost hundreds of dollars. He had it flown especially to Christina, who was in Paris."

He flew to Argentina—and Christina received her breathtakingly lovely doll. It was handed to her by a servant who took it from a messenger at the door.

As Christina grew older, her tastes ran to Pucci dresses and Gucci leather. Her formal education ended after a few months at Queen's College in London; she had showed little interest in school or a career. Much of her time was spent in Paris, dining at Maxim's and the Tour d'Argent and nightclubbing at Castel and Regine's. She knew that her father had set up a trust fund for her and that when she reached twenty-one she would receive one million dollars.

Baron Arnaud de Rosnay, who has known Christina since she was a child, said, "She was given far too much money—a bad mistake. All she had to do was spend."

It was in 1973, in the midst of her despair and

despondency following Alexander's death, that a turning point came in Christina Onassis' life. Ari took her in hand and changed her from an aimless jet-setter who had only vague life goals into a purposeful woman who, with pride in her family, has firmly grasped the reins he dropped.

Newspapers and magazines have described the remarkable change in Christina after her father died. One publication, quoting a friend, wrote, "She has had a modest demeanor all her life, sort of an ugly duckling, the eternal wallflower. Now she looks beautiful. She speaks, acts, and looks like a woman who has been liberated."

Few realize how the transformation was effected.

It was not a sudden change in a woman who, realizing that she now heads a business empire, rises to the challenge by some mysterious force of personality. It was planned, carefully and deliberately, by Aristotle Onassis.

Until 1973, he had named Alexander as his business heir. Christina, whom he loved dearly, was to share the fruits but not the labor of producing them. But when Alexander died, his plans suddenly changed. Christina would be in the seat of power.

Ari, creating a one-pupil university, set about teaching his daughter the complex shipping business, at first tutoring her himself. After an initial period of instruction, he sent her to New York City, where Constantine Gratsos, his elderly but astute chief aide in the United States and the Far East, took her in hand and poured facts about shipping into her. She spent hours each day at his elbow, listening, learning, asking countless questions.

After three months of intense training, she returned to the Monaco headquarters of the empire and went to work, showing up early in the morning, remaining until late, working and learning, Ari counseling her. With her father, she traveled to London, Paris, New York, and other cities, sitting in on important conferences, taking an active role in the discussions and decision-making. George S. Moore, retired chairman of the First National City Bank, says, "She was present at practically every meeting I had with her father after her brother died." He adds, "Christina feels a great sense of trusteeship to the world. She wants to make this fortune count. The last thing in the world she wants is fancy dresses. She wants to carry on her father's work."

Obviously, it will take more than a crash course to instruct Christina in all the facets of the shipping business. But she has taken over with a sureness and astuteness that amazes executives. For example, almost from the start, she realized that her New York City birth presented a tax problem. So she relinquished her American citizenship. Last April, a month after her father died, she signed the necessary documents in the United States consulate in Nice that allowed her to renounce all formal American ties. A battery of lawyers had advised that the action would save millions of dollars in inheritance taxes and that she could still visit the United States regularly as a foreign national. They pointed out that at birth she had automatically become an Argentine citizen because of her father's citizenship there.

The value of the property Christina had inherited may be considerably reduced because, as 1975 drew to a close, the international tanker business was in financial trouble. As Constantine Gratsos puts it, "I've been in it for fifty years. I've seen many crises—this one is a catastrophe." But the shrewd seventy-three-year-old businessman added that he expects the tide to turn in 1980 and quotes a favorite Onassis slogan— "In shipping, the advantage is always to the one with the most patience."

A longtime Onassis competitor observed, "From what I've already seen, that girl has plenty of patience. I predict that she'll behave exactly like her father— wait and pounce."

As her father's marriage took shape, some of the tension between Jackie and Christina abated, and the two drew closer together. Jackie took Christina in hand and set about transforming her appearance. The young girl, aware that Jackie's tastes were impeccable, was a willing pupil.

Jackie personally took her stepdaughter to her own hairdresser, Mary Farr, at Kenneth's in New York, and supervised the creation of a new, more flattering hairdo. She went shopping with her in Paris and Rome. One day, in a Paris boutique, Jackie sat in a green upholstered chair as Christina tried on dresses. Once she emerged in a striped shirtwaist dress that Jackie firmly vetoed. "Oh, no!" she said. "You look like Florence Nightingale in that one. It's not for you." Dutifully, Christina retreated into the dressing room. When she reappeared in a simple white frock, Jackie clapped her hands and said, "Yes, yes! That's you!" Christina glowed.

From then on, the relationship assumed a curious on-again, off-again status. One week, they would be friendly and almost cozy, laughing and obviously enjoying each other's company. The next, there would be an incident like this one. One day, by accident, they were both dining at Maxim's in Paris. Although they were seated at tables near each other, neither spoke to the other. Jackie was the first to leave. She picked up her purse and seemed to stare at the younger woman, but offered no sign of recognition as she swept out of the restaurant. The reason for the rift was unexplained.

None of their friends know for sure what would draw them together or what would cause the sparks to fly. One perceptive woman puts it thus. "Each is a mercurial human being, responding to her emotions of the moment." Another friend, also noting the odd turn-abouts, shook her head in perplexity as she said, "When I was eight years old, I had a toy called a ric-rac, consisting of a wooden racket and a tiny rubber ball. The idea was to hit the ball in the air. Up and down, up and down, up and down. Jackie and Christina are just like that ball!"

In 1972, *Life* magazine reported that Christina had said, "It's not true what all the papers write—that Jackie bosses him and he is her slave. It is just the opposite. She always tries to please him in everything. Whenever they are together she seems to fall more in love with him. She's always asking what she can do for him. If I had to choose, I'd say that my father is more important to Jackie than vice versa."

She added, "Jackie is my stepmother, but also my friend. Once, she was going through a difficult period with my father. But I didn't want to get mixed up in their personal affairs and said it would be better if they could solve their problems alone. When I saw her some time later, she told me everything that had happened. She was very wrought up and needed to talk to someone, to a good and close friend. That is what we are to each other."

After Alexander's death, Christina was grateful to Jackie for trying to cheer her grieving father. She said at the time, "Jackie knows the meaning of tragedy and is doing everything humanly possible to help him. I'm so very thankful to her."

However, the ball dropped when Ari became ill. Christina felt that her stepmother wasn't doing enough to help him. Ari's private nurse said that the two women were often with Ari in the hospital, but would sit at opposite ends of the room and not speak to each other.

"At the funeral on Skorpios," said a relative, "they made a pretense to normalcy, but Christina was very upset with Jackie. They started out in the same car, but after they had gone a short distance, Christina got out and transferred to another auto."

An added reason for the coolness was supposed to have been caused by Ted Kennedy. Friends of the Onassis family said that at the time of the funeral, Ted, who also attended, had tried to speak to Christina about financial matters.

Their relations reached a low ebb after the death of Onassis, when it was believed that Jackie might contest the will. Reports reached Christina that Jackie was marshaling an army of legal talent in pursuit of the multimillion-dollar fortune. Both women were in London in early May and both checked in at the posh Claridge's Hotel, but they saw each other in London only briefly at the offices of an American lawyer. The meeting was cold and tense. In a few hours, Jackie was en route to Athens, while Christina remained in London for conferences with executives and associates of the shipping empire.

But the titanic clash many predicted never occurred. The ball bounced up again at Christina's second wedding in the summer of 1975.

After Ari's death, it was widely assumed that Christina would marry Peter Goulandris, scion of a Greek shipping dynasty. There was much talk that she had promised her father on his deathbed to make such an alliance. She put that story to rest when she issued a statement in which she said, "I'm not going to marry Peter. Not because it's too soon after my father's death, but because I don't have plans to marry him or anyone else."

She changed her mind quickly. In July 1975, she married for the second time. Ari would have approved of her choice—the bridegroom was thirty-one-year-old Alexander Andreadis, the husky, dark-haired heir to one of the great banking and shipping fortunes in Greece. The young man had once given Onassis a tip on the purchase of gold that resulted in netting Ari a quick profit of millions of dollars.

Christina had met Alexander at the Athens Hilton—the young man's father is the major stockholder in the hotel. The meeting had been arranged by Christina's aunt, but we were told, "They're both stubborn young people, and if they didn't like each other enough to get married, they would have gone in opposite directions. It may not have been love at first sight, but they weren't wearing blinders or veils either!"

Andreadis' father, Stratis, is a self-made multimillionaire and former law professor. He is known to be a very practical man who believes that it's good business to be on the winning side. His friends tell a story, doubtless apocryphal, to prove this point. He was backing a candidate for prime minister, but on election day, his man appeared to be losing decisively. So he hopped into his chauffeur-driven limousine and went rapidly to the winner's headquarters. He burst in smiling and cheering. "We won! We won!" he shouted.

Christina's husband is the grandson of a former head

of government. Alexander's maternal grandfather, for whom he was named, was Alexander Koryz, premier of Greece when the Nazis invaded the country in 1941. The young man graduated from Zurich University with honors in mechanical engineering. He is regarded as a shrewd businessman and is currently the managing director of Greece's largest ship repair yard, owned by his father.

Father Marius Bapergolas, who has known Alexander since childhood, conducted the wedding ceremony. He said, "Alexander doesn't just sit with his feet up, gobbling up his father's money. He's far from lazy."

The wedding was held in a tiny seaside chapel in Glyfada. The chapel, which held only twenty-five guests, was decorated to resemble a Byzantine monastery of the fifteenth century.

Because the church was so small, Christina and her aunts had to carefully check and recheck the guest list. One of the first to receive an invitation was Jackie. Christina sent her personal plane to Athens to fetch her stepmother.

"Everything was so sudden," said Christina's Aunt Artemis Garoufalides. "She is very happy, because, for the first time, she has found a man who really loves her."

In Washington, a sour note was sounded by twenty-four-year-old Denis Sioris, daughter of a U.S. diplomat, who said, "I was shocked. *I* was going with him up to a week ago."

And Jackie? She said she would be delighted to attend the wedding. Christina clapped her hands joyously when she heard. At the wedding, the two women kissed and hugged and laughed. At the reception afterward, Jackie was at Christina's side much of the time. When she circulated among the other guests, she spoke animatedly about Christina's radiance. One guest said, "It was as though she had raised Christina herself and now, as mother of the bride, was all aglow with happiness at her daughter's wedding."

After the ceremony, Jackie talked with newsmen. "I so love that child," she said, "and I am happy that she has found him. At last I can see happy days ahead for her."

And Christina said, "I'm so lucky to have her as my stepmother and friend."

Given their natures and the circumstances of their lives, there is no guarantee that the euphoria will continue. But it can be said that the so-called deadly feud reported between the two women is ended. Jackie is no longer a threat to Christina. Her marriage to Christina's father has been ended by death, and she has made no move to claim a large share of the Onassis fortune. What might have become a monumental struggle between the two women over the many millions Onassis left has apparently been averted.

Christina is happily married, and Jackie is an international jet-setter once again, no longer closely involved with the Onassis family, and so there is peace.

Epilogue

Spring was a time of numbness; summer was for reflection and planning a new life. When September came, Jackie began again.

"I'm going to be very busy this fall," she announced to Nancy Tuckerman, her social secretary in the White House and a close friend. To Dave Powers, a former White House aide who has also remained a family intimate, she confided that she will fill her time "doing things that really matter."

This is what it was like for her as she set about remaking her life.

She helped Caroline shop for clothes and pack for her year at Sotheby's in England.

She journeyed up to Waltham, Massachusetts where John F. Kennedy memorabilia is housed in a temporary center until the memorial library is built. With Powers, who is now acting curator of the library, she went through the cavernous two-story high room. Here, hundreds of paintings of the president are hung on the walls and stacked on shelves; there are dozens of busts, the ship models he treasured, his handwritten scrimshaw, the coconut shell on which he scratched a message for help when his PT boat was sunk. From the many thousands of relics, she began selecting the personal ones that will eventually be housed in the museum. Slowly, she walked with Powers around the huge room, her eyes misting over when she picked up items she recognized as having meant a great deal to the late president.

She began active work on two projects that have captured her interest. One is a campaign to prevent demolition of Grand Central Terminal; another, a campaign to restore Newport, Rhode Island to its former elegance. She is active, too, in the International Center of Photography, which is housed in the former Fifth Avenue home of the National Audubon Society not far from her New York apartment. The center holds photography exhibitions, teaches the art, and creates archives to preserve photographs.

She closets herself in her Fifth Avenue home for long periods of time, writing. She wouldn't say what, but Nancy Tuckerman told us, "She is positively *not* writing her memoirs, as has been reported." (A short article she wrote about the photography center was published in January 1975 in *The New Yorker*. The magazine's Brendan Gill believes Jackie has promise as a writer.)

In mid-September 1975, she went to work for Viking Press in New York as an editorial consultant. Her job, according to Thomas H. Guinzburg, the company's president, includes scouting for possible manuscripts from her "wide circle of social, political, and international contacts." While Jackie has been given an office at the publishing house, she has no prescribed hours of work; much of the time, she works from her home. Guinzberg, too, scotched reports that she was writing her memoirs. "As far as I know," he said, "she has no present plan to write a book herself."

Still an ardent horsewoman, she had added a new exercise hobby—jogging. She takes off from upper Fifth Avenue, sometimes in early morning, sometimes around noon, and jogs around the lake in Central Park.

Reports have been published that she plans to start a stud farm and raise thoroughbreds on an estate she owns in New Jersey hunt country. A British newspaper said, "She has told friends that she will retire from the public arena and take up the day-to-day management of a business for the first time in her life since she married President Kennedy and gave up work for a newspaper." Nancy Tuckerman chuckles when she hears the story. "It's untrue," she says.

Marriage plans? It's a nationwide guessing game, and anyone can play. Her escorts following Ari's death have included Cary Grant, Warren Beatty, Senator John Tunney, Truman Capote, Frank Sinatra, Rudolf Nureyev, and Dr. Christiaan Barnard. Another current friend is a forty-five-year-old bachelor named Karl Katz. Last July, Jackie invited Katz, the director of special projects at New York's Metropolitan Museum of Art, to spend several days with her on Skorpios.

Katz is a Brooklyn-born son of a wool wholesaler and had been regarded as a boy-wonder in the art world. For eleven years he was the director of Jerusalem's Bezalel National Museum. In 1968, he took over as director of New York's Jewish Museum and three years later came to the Metropolitan. Katz denies that he's a potential suitor and says, "There is not even a basis for this rumor in quicksand. It's absurd."

After Ari died, Jacqueline appraised herself in midlife. She was the widow of two of the world's most prominent and powerful men and she was only forty-five years old. She was also still beautiful; she still had her glamor image, and she was still the most talked-about woman in the world. The tantalizing question has to be—what new sensation will she cause, with what man, in what setting? For Jacqueline Kennedy Onassis, we can be certain, will not fade into obscurity.

As for her incredible marriage with Aristotle Onassis, she summed it up herself a few months after he died.

"He rescued me at a moment when my life was engulfed in shadows," she told the Athens newspaper, *Eleftheros Cosmos*. "He brought me into a world where one could find both happiness and love. We lived through many beautiful experiences together, which cannot be forgotten and for which I will be eternally grateful to him."

The following is the text of Aristotle Onassis' last will and testament.

"My Will"

Article 1 (First). "If my death occurs before I proceed with the establishment of a Cultural Institution in Vaduz, Lichtenstein, or elsewhere under the name of 'ALEXANDER ONASSIS FOUNDATION,' its purpose being among others, to operate, maintain and promote the Nursing, Educational, Literary Works, Religious, Scientific research, Journalistic and Artistic endeavors, proclaiming International or National Contests, prize awards in money, similar to the plan of the NOBEL Institution in Sweden, I entrust and command the undersigned executors of my will to establish such a Cultural Institution in Vaduz, Lichtenstein or elsewhere keeping the aforementioned purpose in mind or similar ones or some others of their own choice agreed upon after taking vote among themselves and after arranging for the Charter governing the said Institution. I wish that all the aforesaid commands of the present Will be carried out by the said Institution regardless of whether it has in the meanwhile been built by me or it will be built by the executors of this Will after my death."

THE STOCKS OF THE COMPANIES

Article 2 (Second). "I wish that all the stocks of my Maritime and other Companies residing in Panama, the Republic of Panama or elsewhere be transferred under absolute ownership to the Company that will be built by me or the executors of my Will, in Panama or elsewhere which will own one thousand shares without nominative value and exercise full control over the rest of the Companies, which for the purpose of distinction in the present Will I will name it for the time being Company 'B'.

"Also, I wish to proceed in the establishment of another Company in Panama or elsewhere with holdings up to one thousand anonymous shares without nominative value, which will exercise full control on the rest of the Companies and which for purposes of distinction from the others, I will name it in this Will for the time being, Company 'A'. To this Company 'A', it is necessary that the 950 (nine hundred fifty) shares of Company 'B' be transferred by absolute ownership in such a way that all the Maritime Companies residing in Panama or elsewhere to be controlled by the Company 'B' which is going to be built in the future and will be fully controlled by the Company 'A'.

"I wish that I be, in relation to the companies, owner of the 1,000 (one thousand) on top of one thousand shares of Company 'A' and owner of 50 (fifty) shares on top of one thousand shares of Company 'B' and the ownership of all the shares out of the rest of Maritime or other Companies to devolve upon the Company 'B' as mentioned above. I wish that the commands given in the present Will be carried out as if the said Companies 'A' and 'B' have already been founded, and if my death occurs before they are built, I entrust and command through the present Will the undersigned executors of my will to build Companies 'A' and 'B' and transfer the shares of all the Companies in Panama or elsewhere to these before they proceed in the distribution of my Fortune elements to my heirs and execute the rest of my Commands expressed in the present Will."

JACQUELINE

Article 3 (Third). "Having already taken care of my wife Jacqueline Bouvier and having extracted a written agreement through Notary in U.S.A. by which she gives up her hereditary rights on my inheritance, I limit share for her and her two children John and Caroline Kennedy to a lifelong income of $150,000 in U.S.A. Here is the record in detail: If she (my wife) or her heirs lay claim to my inheritance for a larger share than the aforementioned lifelong income, I command the executors of my Will and the rest of my heirs that they deny her such a right through all legal means, cost and expenses charged on my inheritance. But if she is accidentally entitled to such a share through final Court decision non-susceptible of offense through regular or special legal means, I limit her share to ⅛ (one eighth) of my hereditary Fortune taken out of my daughter Christina's hereditary share decreasing the latter's lot proportionately.

"In that case I leave to my wife namely: 1) one quarter of the shares out of every Company, VICTORY CARRIERS of New York, and VICTORY DEVELOPMENTS of New York out of which 25% (twenty five per cent) belongs to the Panamaic Company ARIONA which in turn belongs to me completely. And 75% (seventy five per cent) through TRUST revokable by me. 2) A total of 12 (twelve) Stocks out of the 50 ones (fifty) which are under my ownership held by the future Company 'B'. 3) A total of 112.50 (one hundred twelve and a half) shares held by the future Company 'A' out of its total of one thousand. 4) 15% (fifteen per cent) out of 90% (ninety per cent) Stock holdings of Olympic Airways which are under my ownership, 10% out of the shares of Olympic Airways to my cousin Konstantinos Konialides. And 5) ¼ (one quarter) out of the rest of my inheritance comprised of furniture, valuables and rest of movable objects."

CHRISTINA

Article 4 (Fourth). "A) In case that my wife Jacqueline inherits nothing more as a result of her agreement I limit the hereditary share of daughter Christina born out of the legal matrimony to Athena Livanos, to the following: 1) A total of 4/4 (four quarters) of all the Stocks held by VICTORY CARRIERS & VICTORY DEVELOPMENTS of New York, out of which 25% (twenty-five per cent) belong to the Panamaic Company of ARIONA which in turn belongs completely to me, and 75% (seventy-five per cent) through TRUST revokable by me. 2) 50 (fifty) shares held by the Company 'B'. 3) 450 (four hundred and fifty) shares held by Company 'A'. 4) 61% (sixty-one per cent) out of the 90% (ninety per cent) holdings of Olympic Airways which are under my ownership. 5) The totality of the rest of my hereditary Estate comprised of Furniture, valuables and all the rest of the movable objects.

"B) In case my wife Jacqueline by final and irrevokable legal decision is entitled of hereditary Share in spite of her resignation from all hereditary rights, then I limit my daughter Christina to ⅜ (three eighths) of the hereditary Estate, especially I leave her the following: 1) the ¾ (three quarters) of the shares held by VICTORY CARRIERS of New York and VICTORY DEVELOPMENTS of New York. 2) 38 (thirty-eight) shares out of the Company 'B'. 3) 337.5 (three hundred thirty seven and a half) shares held by Company 'A'. 4) The ¾ (three quarters) of the rest of the hereditary Estate comprised by Furniture, Valuables and the rest of all movable objects."

PART II

THE OBLIGATIONS OF THE HEIRS

Article 5 (Fifth). "To the future non-profit (Cultural) Foundation under the title of 'ALEXANDER ONASSIS FOUNDATION,' I leave: 1) 550 (five hundred fifty) shares on a total of one thousand of the Company 'A'. 2) 39% (thirty-nine per cent) of the 90% (ninety per cent) of the Olympic Airways shares."

Article 6 (Sixth). "I wish that my heirs, including the Foundation, be charged with the following obligations, that is: from the revenues and incomes of any kind out of every Company of mine the following sums be paid according to the priorities and order which I determine. 1) Above all to deduct the general expenses, service expenses, exploitation, maintenance, etc., all kinds of burdens, expenses and expenditures of all my companies. 2) Next, to deduct all kinds of debts, interests, mortgage payments and the rest of every kind of demands which burden these companies and especially the ships, airplanes, moveables and immoveables. I [would] like to make clear here that if the mortgage payments of each Concrete Estate element is not in a financial position to make its own mortgage payments out of its own profits but it is covered by the revenues of the other Estate element or by savings or loans of other Estate element then it is necessary that a 6–10% (six to ten per cent) be deducted annually out of the revenues of this particular Estate element until its full liquidation. 3) Out of the rest of the Estate the following lifelong sums should be paid to: 1) My daughter Christina, $250,000 (two hundred fifty thousand dollars) annually, and if she marries, her husband gets $50,000 (fifty thousand dollars) annually as long as he lives. 2) [To] my wife Jacqueline $100,000 dollars (one hundred thousand dollars) to her alone and $25,000 (twenty-five thousand dollars) annually to each of her children John and Caroline Kennedy—until they complete their 21 (twenty-first) years of age. When this completion of 21 (twenty-first) happens, the sums destined for them should fall to the lot of my wife so that she gets finally $150,000 (one hundred fifty thousand dollars) annually, which after [they] are added to the income of $100,000 (one hundred thousand dollars) bonds annually clear of tax, secure a total of $250,000 (two hundred fifty thousand dollars) annual income. The abovementioned sums for both my wife and my daughter should be readjusted every three years taking into consideration the cost of living of the year 1973 so that the buying value [will] stay as much as possible at the level of the buying value of the year 1973. 3) My sisters. To each of my sisters, Artemis Garofalides, Merope Konialides and Kalliroe Patronikola $60,000 (sixty thousand dollars) annually for life. And these Sums will be readjusted as in the case of my daughter's and my wife's mentioned above. 4) To my cousins from father's and mother's side $50,000 (fifty thousand dollars) annually proportionately distributed among them, according to their needs, not more than $5,000 (five thousand dollars) annually each—under the absolute judgment of my sister Artemis Garofalides; after her death, my sister Kalliroe Patronikola; and after her death, under the judgment of the closest relative. Since I have taken care of the rest of my relations in the same manner, especially of my cousins, Nicholas Konialides and Konstantinos Konialides, consequently I leave nothing to them. 5) Respectively to the above mentioned future Institution 'ALEXANDER ONASSIS FOUNDATION' will invested the minimum Sum of U.S.A. $1,000,000 (one million dollars) annually after the sums for the investments as will be in turn worked out. If the proportionate surpluses of exploitation or dividends coming from the stocks invested in the Foundation are larger than one million dollars ($1,000,000) and in some year happens to be lower than one million dollars ($1,000,000) and since this Sum will have been Supplemented through loans or down payments, then it will be returned to the Companies through down payments or supplemented through any means Sum coming from the Foundation's other uses surpluses exceeding this minimum Sum of one million U.S.A. dollars ($1,000,000) annually. 6) From the balance of surpluses or dividends a rate of 50% (fifty per cent) up to 60% (sixty per cent) will be deducted for investments or contra-investments and a rate of 10%

(ten per cent) for savings. 7) My collaborators. Afterwards, out of the rest of the following collaborators will be paid the following sums annually, on condition that they continue rendering their services to the Caucus of my companies and only released of their obligations in case of illness or disability, on top of their salary they get for their Services, that is: a) To my cousin Konstantinos Konialides the sum of $60,000 (sixty thousand U.S.A. dollars) annually. I [would] like to make clear that the latter already receives the sum of $200,000 (two hundred thousand dollars) annually as salary for his services. b) To my collaborators Konstantinos Gratsos, Nicholas Kokkinis, Stylianos Papademetriou and Michael Dollaglore $30,000 (thirty thousand dollars) each annually. c) To my collaborators Konstantinos Vdassopoulos and Anastasius Konnondes $20,000 (twenty thousand dollars) for each one of them annually. d) To my collaborators Panagiotis Nikolaides, GREOR BREVEN and Andreas Spyrou $12,000 (twelve thousand dollars) for each annually. e) To my collaborators Paul Soannides, Apostalos Zambelas, Haralambus Navrokefalos, Christos Kapetanakeo, Miltiados Giannakopoulos, Captain Konstantinos Anastasiados and Gerusimos Dragonas $6,000 (six thousand dollars) each annually. From the rest of the balance I command the payments for the members of my governing Council of the Foundation and my companies Athena Livanos-Niarchos, Christina Onassis, my wife Jacqueline, Konstantinos Konialides, Nicholas Kokkinis, Konstantinos Gratsos, Stylianos Papademetriou, Kanstantinos Vlussopoulos, Michael Dollaglore, ROGER LOUBERY, Paul Ioannides and Apostalos Zambelas, all of whom I appoint as permanent members of the governing Council of the future non-profit (Cultural) Foundation, and a rate of 2%

(two per cent) out of the whatever kind clear surpluses realized by all companies after deduction of the sums written in the paragraphs from 1–7 (one to seven) of the above Article 6 (six) of the present Will, on the condition that there *are* such surpluses and on the condition that they will continue to render their services to the Foundation, distributed among themselves at equal parts. In case of death, resignation, illness or some disability among some of them, the rest will appoint by majority vote his substitute who will be entitled to the proportion of the substitute. In case that 10/12 (ten twelfths) of the members of the governing Council either of the non-profit (Cultural) Foundation or the companies deem correct that some member among them does not work to his full capacity like the others and under the absolute judgment of the majority of 10/12 (ten twelfths) of the members, this majority is entitled to ask for the immediate resignation of the uncooperative member and that he is obligated to give in and leave the governing Council without Compensation or any claim or demand."

PART III

"8) The rest of the balance after the deduction of all the above mentioned Sums from one to seven 1–7 of Article 6 (six) of the present Will, should be considered as clear surplus and be distributed to my heirs and to the foundation according to the command given to them through the present 'Will.' "

"9) It becomes clear here that in case the revenues and the rest of every kind of incomes and Surpluses are not sufficient to cover the sums mentioned in the paragraphs one, two, three, four and five (1, 2, 3, 4 and 5) of Article 6 (six) of the present 'Will,' then these Sums will be covered in part or wholly and if possibly by the Savings, if these exist, or by borrowing or by selling of Estate elements of Such Value that it merely covers in this way strictly the arising shortage. Consequently the time of payment of the sums mentioned in the paragraphs 6, 7, 8, 9 and 10 (six, seven, eight, nine, ten) will be extended until and when and if they will exist in the future such surpluses exceeding the coverage, in turn and according to the priority, if the sums mentioned in the paragraphs from 1 through 5 (one through five) of Article 6 (six) of the present 'Will' are sufficient for the coverage in part or wholly of the rest foreseeable sums of the paragraphs 6, 7, 8, 9 (six, seven, eight, nine) of Article 6 (six) of the present 'Will.' "

PERSONNEL AND ATTENDANTS

Article 7 (Seventh). "To the following collaborators, staff and attending personnel I command that they be paid 60 days after my death the total amount of $170,000 (one hundred seventy thousand U.S.A. dollars), distributed among them once and for all on the condition that they resign simultaneously in writing from every claim, of any nature, against me, my heirs, my companies and the foundation, from any cause until the date of my death, else he will receive nothing whoever among them does not comply with the above mentioned commands.

"To Demetrios Vlismas $20,000 (twenty thousand U.S.A. dollars). To P. Cristcelon $10,000 (ten thousand U.S.A. dollars). To K. Dervis $20,000 (twenty thousand U.S.A. dollars). To Stephanos Lafonzos $15,000 (fifteen thousand U.S.A. dollars). To Achilles Kupsambelis $15,000 (fifteen thousand U.S.A. dollars). To CHARLES ROSAU $20,000 (twenty thousand U.S.A. dollars). To PAULA BICEN $10,000 (ten thousand U.S.A. dollars). To JEAN BARRALES $10,000 (ten thousand U.S.A. dollars). To George Syron $20,000 (twenty thousand U.S.A. dollars). To Georgia Beta $5,000 (five thousand U.S.A. dollars). To Panugiotis Konidates $5,000 (five thousand U.S.A. dollars)."

MY YACHT

Article 8 (Eighth). "My Yacht 'Christina,' if my daughter and my wife so wish, they can keep for their own personal use if they are in a position to pay out of their own incomes the annual expenses for its motion and maintenance, amounting to about $500,000 (five hundred thousand U.S.A. dollars) annually. Otherwise, I command that after they take their proportion —¾ (three quarters) [for] my daughter and ¼ (one quarter [for] my wife—whatever objects of their liking from the furniture and the rest of moveable things and after they substitute these by copies or whatever else seems possible, be given to the Greek Treasury for the personal use of every new leader of the Greek state."

Article 9 (Ninth). "As for the small islands of Skorpios and Sparti and the establishments that are on them, if my daughter and my wife so wish they can preserve them for their own personal use if and after they can cover out of their own money the annual expenses of maintenance, amounting to the Sum of about $100,000 (one hundred thousand U.S.A. dollars). Otherwise I command that they be given as a gift to the Olympic Airways for the personal use of its staff, as holiday resorts and especially for children's encampments under the name of "Gift of Alexander Onassis." Excluded from this donation is the 30 (thirty) acre area around the existing chapel and tomb of my son Alexander Onassis, preserving this as a monument. The above-mentioned donation to Olympic Airways is Subject to the following condition: The island of Skorpios will be given as a gift to the Greek Treasury—first and preferably as a holiday resort for the use of every new leader of the Greek State on the condition that the Treasury would undertake its maintenance. If the Treasury accepts the gift then the small island of Sparti will be given as a gift to Olympic Airlines to be used as a holiday resort for its staff and especially as a Summer children's shelter for their children. If the Treasury refuses to accept the gift of Skorpios then both islands, Sparti and Skorpios, will come under the ownership of Olympic Airlines."

[Article 10 is a lengthy and involved explanation of how the governing council of the Alexander Onassis Foundation should be set up, and of the rights and duties of its members.—THE AUTHORS]

Article 11 (Eleventh). "If my daughter and my wife decline the inheritance which I have brought about to them through my present 'Will' or will rebate it, I will leave the share of each one of them and the brought about part of my Estate, to the above foundation of 'ALEXANDER ONASSIS FOUNDATION' which will be built by me or by the executors of my Will. When my daughter dies childless—even though she be married— the shares left to her through the present Will [shall] fall under the lot of the Foundation which will be built, according to what was said above; the same applies to my wife Jacqueline too, even if she is married and her children outlive her."

THE EXECUTION OF THE WILL

Article 12 (Twelfth). "Co-executors of my 'Will.' I assign the mother of my son Alexander, Athena née St. Livanos-Onassis-BLANDFORD-Niarchos, my daughter Christina A. Onassis, Konstantinos Konialides, Nicholas Kokkinis, Stylianos Papademetriou, Michael Dollaglore, who, together and collectively acting, will look after the carrying out of my last Wish. If any one of them dies or decline my mandate, the rest of them will elect through majority his substitute. . . . The mother of my son Alexander, Athena, née Livanos-Onassis-BLAND-FORD-Niarchos I command to preside over the co-executors of my 'Will.' The abovementioned co-executors of my 'Will' are ordered and authorized through money and expenses out of my inherited Estate to exhaust all legal and judicial margins for the carrying out of the commands of my present 'Will,' and against any offense no matter where it comes from."

Article 13 (Thirteenth). "If, before my death occurs, I contract agreement of 'gratis' cause of death between me, my daughter Christina and my wife Jacqueline or the foundation which will be built, by virtue of which I will transfer to them all my Estate elements, I wish that the present 'Will' be considered as nonexistent."

Article 14 (Fourteenth). "Every offense against my 'Will' by a person mentioned in it, relative or not, I command that it have as a result the suspension of the commands of my 'Will' in relation to him only and until the final court decision of the dispute. Every previous 'Will' of mine is revoked by the present one which I wrote in my own handwriting from the beginning to the end in New York or rather on the private airplane "Lear" from Acapulco of Mexico to New York, on Thursday between the hours 4 and 10 P.M., January 3rd (third) of the year 1974 (nineteen hundred seventy-four) and I signed as follows: ARISTOTELES SOCRATES ONASSIS."

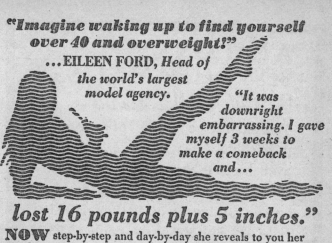

"Imagine waking up to find yourself over 40 and overweight!"

...EILEEN FORD, *Head of the world's largest model agency.*

"It was downright embarrassing. I gave myself 3 weeks to make a comeback and...

lost 16 pounds plus 5 inches."

NOW step-by-step and day-by-day she reveals to you her own beautifying plan in her new book, *Eileen Ford's A More Beautiful You in 21 Days*. The plan uses everything she knows about—

EXERCISE—not boring and repetitive, but a pleasant, varied program that you can do in a few minutes.

DIET—delicious, slimming menus and recipes for 21 days for you and your family from the world's best restaurants.

BEAUTY CARE—How to cure The Frizzies. First aid and lasting beauty for fingernails and hands. Quick make-up magic. The secret to a sexy voice. How to make the most of your assets. And many, many more.

You have nothing to lose but inches and years!

At your bookstore or mail this coupon now for free 10-day trial

---

SIMON AND SCHUSTER, Dept. 61, 630 Fifth Ave., N.Y. 10020
Please send my copy of *Eileen Ford's A More Beautiful You in 21 Days*. If I'm not convinced that it can help me, I may return it within 10 days and owe nothing. Otherwise, I will send $9.95 plus mailing as payment in full.

(Please Print)

Name_____

Address_____

City_____State_____Zip_____

☐ SAVE POSTAGE. Check here if you enclose check or money order for the books you want—then we pay postage. 10-day trial privilege guarantee holds.

☐ Also please send *"Eileen Ford's Book of Model Beauty,"* at $9.95. Money back guarantee if not delighted.

S75/3A